School Law

A California Perspective

Arthur J. Townley
June Schmieder-Ramirez
Kenneth E. Lane
Lillian B. Wehmeyer

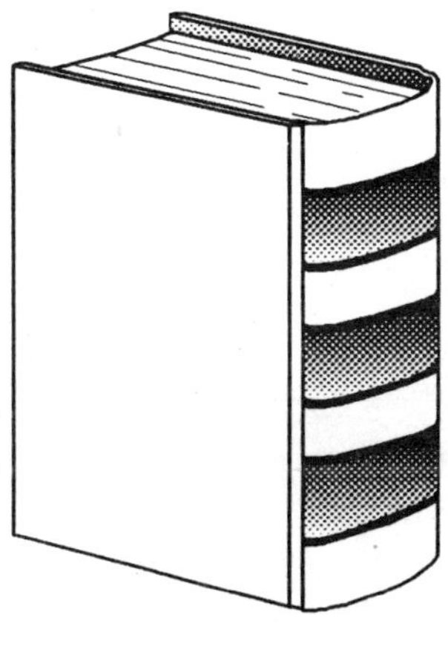

KENDALL/HUNT PUBLISHING COMPANY
4050 Westmark Drive Dubuque, Iowa 52002

This text is a general guide to legal aspects of education in California. Every effort was made to ensure that it was up-to-date at the time of publication. This book is not intended to serve as a guide to action in specific situations and does not in any way substitute for the advice of an attorney.

The authors:

Arthur J. Townley

Professor Emeritus, School of Education, California State University, San Bernardino

June Schmieder-Ramirez

Professor, School of Education & Psychology, Pepperdine University, California

Kenneth E. Lane

Professor, School of Education, California State University, San Bernardino

Lillian B. Wehmeyer

Professor, School of Education & Behavioral Studies, Azusa Pacific University, California

ISBN 0-7872-8675-3

Printed in the United States of America
10 9 8 7 6 5 4 3 2 1

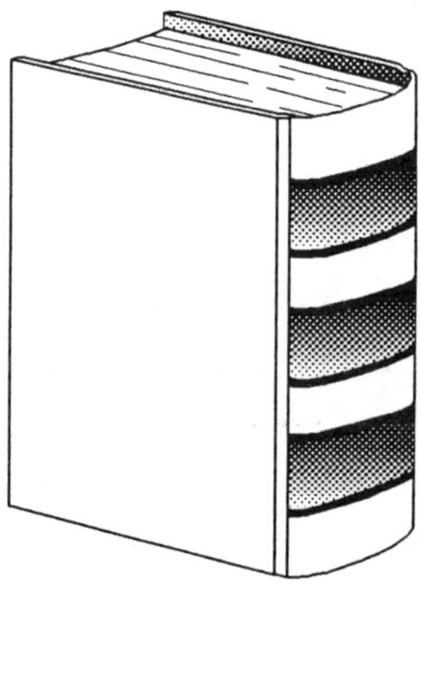

Table of Contents

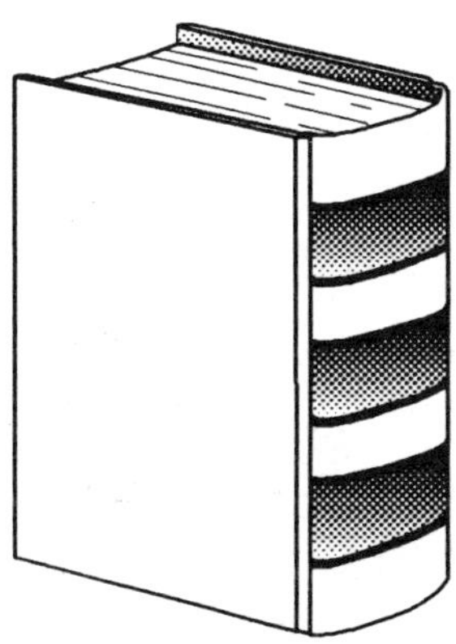

Preface

The authors are pleased to present the first edition of *School Law: A California Perspective*, a textbook designed for students who are completing an administrative credential or graduate degree in educational administration. It can also serve as a reference for those teachers and administrators who are currently serving in a school leadership role. The authors found a variety of law books written from a national perspective, but saw need for an education law book emphasizing those critical issues confronting California educators. The objective of this text is to fulfill that need.

Any author of a school law text faces the formidable task of selecting those topics, legislation, and court decisions that are most relevant in the current school setting. Drawing on our collective experience of more than 70 years as teachers and administrators in California public education, this text offers a practical and realistic perspective of school law for students and administrators.

The text discusses the relevant laws and court decisions that will assist administrators and teachers in making decisions about students, personnel issues, curriculum and instruction, fiscal and legal matters, and copyright. Given the dynamic nature of the law, no single text can serve to keep school personnel abreast of the most recent legislation and court decisions. However, familiarity with the underlying principles of legislation and court decisions will give school personnel more confidence in dealing with legal questions.

The information in this text will serve as a guide for teachers and administrators as they provide leadership to schools, but it is not intended to serve as a substitute for legal counsel. Educators confronting legal problems should always seek the advice of a competent attorney.

We are committed to continued development and refinement of this textbook. To that end, we invite feedback from instructors of courses in education law. We encourage you to give us the benefit of your input and that of your students. We encourage proposals, not only for revisions or additions to existing chapters, but also for new or supplemental material, even entire chapters. If you are interested in improving or contributing to the next edition, please contact one of the authors by e-mail:

Dr. Townley at atownle2@juno.com or Dr. Wehmeyer at lwehmeyer@apu.edu

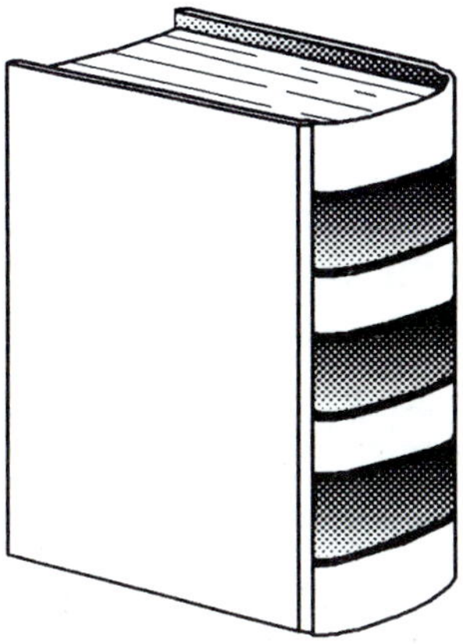

Chapter 1

Sources of School Law

Introduction

The beginning school administrator soon finds that the laws governing education are complex and difficult to interpret—but extremely important. For example, a new assistant principal, during her first day on the job, is told by a student that another student has drugs in her locker. Can the assistant principal, based on this information, search the locker and look for the drugs? Should she call the police and ask them to search the locker? Or should she attempt to find other evidence of drugs before she takes direct action?

As she considers her decision, the assistant principal may try to remember whether, in her school law class, she learned where to find legal information about proper procedures in such a situation. Unfortunately, no single book is likely to offer a clear directive.

School law has many sources. *Black's Law Dictionary* (1999) defines the "law of the land" as "the aggregate of legislation, judicial precedents, and accepted legal principles; the body of authoritative grounds of judicial and administrative action." The California Civil Code (section 22) defines law as "a solemn expression of the will of the supreme power of the State." This supreme power, or controlling authority, is derived from several sources: the federal Constitution, state constitutions, statutes passed by federal and state legislative bodies, and court decisions. This chapter reviews those sources.

The U. S. Constitution and Education

The United States Constitution is the highest level of law in this country. It was written broadly so as to endure changing times and circumstances. While the

Constitution can be changed by amendments, the process is difficult and seldom utilized. Although written more than 200 years ago, the Constitution has been amended only 26 times—and ten of those amendments came into effect shortly after the Constitution was ratified in 1789.

What does the federal Constitution say about education? Nothing! Therefore, education is a function of the state. Why not a function of the local community or of the federal government? The answer lies in the Constitution itself. Nowhere is the word "education" mentioned. Therefore, the Tenth Amendment to the Constitution answers the question. This amendment states, "The powers not delegated to the United States by the Constitution, nor prohibited by it to the States, are reserved to the States respectively, or to the people."

Although provision for education is thus established as one of the powers reserved to the states, the Supremacy Clause of the Constitution (Article VI, Section 2) declares that the Constitution and the laws enacted by the U.S. Congress "in pursuance thereof" are the supreme law of the land. Thus, all statutes passed by Congress, state constitutions and statutes, and policies of local boards of education are subject to and may not violate the provisions of the federal Constitution. The portions of the Constitution that have had the greatest impact on the operation of public schools are Article 1, Sections 8 and 10, and Amendments 1, 4, 5, 8, 10, and 14. Nearly always, one or more of these Constitutional provisions serve as the basis for education-related cases taken to federal courts.

On the other hand, one must keep in mind that although education is a function of the states, the federal government exerts considerable influence in educational issues. This influence on the part of the federal government has come primarily through the provisions of the Constitution just enumerated, decisions of the U.S. Supreme Court, and acts of Congress.

The General Welfare Clause (Article 1, Section 8)

Article 1 of the U.S. Constitution grants Congress "power to lay and collect taxes . . . and provide for the common defense and general welfare of the United States." This provision is based on the assumption that a high level of education is essential for the civic and economic prosperity of a democratic nation—the general welfare. Congress relies on this article when it passes federal statutes and provides federal tax dollars for school programs. The courts have generally upheld the power of Congress to authorize taxes and expenditures related to the general welfare of the United States—including education. Courts have ruled that:

- Intelligence is commerce as defined in the Constitution, and Congress has a right to regulate it (*Gibbons v. Ogden*, 1824)
- Congress is not limited in the expenditure of public monies to the direct or express grants of legislative power found in the Constitution (*United States v. Butler*, 1936)
- Congress can tax and spend under the General Welfare Clause (*Helvering v. Davis*, 1937).

Congress, utilizing its authority under the General Welfare Clause, has enacted a body of legislation to promote and support education. Federal statutes have provided extensive education programs for pre-schoolers through adults in such areas as defense education, vocational programs, math, and science. Legislation has also been enacted to promote civil rights and prohibit sex discrimination. Statutes have authorized services for students whose primary language is not English and for those with special learning difficulties. In addition, Congress has approved legislation designed to protect the confidentiality of pupil records and to eliminate bias against pregnant students. Other funds from the federal government have been directed to such purposes as free and reduced-cost food programs, student transportation, Native American education, and establishment of the military academies.

These laws have generally been upheld by the U.S. Supreme Court, which has interpreted the General Welfare Clause as authorizing Congress to tax and to spend money for a variety of educational activities. However, the Court has not given Congress authority to do anything it pleases to provide for the general welfare—only to tax for such purposes. Therefore, while Congress may levy taxes to provide support for education, it may not legislate control of education (Webb, Metha, & Jordan, 1996).

Obligation of Contracts Clause (Article 1, Section 10)

The Obligation of Contracts Clause in the U.S. Constitution provides in part that no state may "pass any . . . law impairing the obligation of contracts." Court decisions have affirmed that contracts entered into by school districts are fully protected. Examples include personnel contracts and other contracted services. This provision of the Constitution prohibits a state legislature, for example, from passing a law detrimental to a teacher who has acquired contractual status under existing statutes. Specifically, the obligation provision comes into play if a state legislature seeks to alter a teacher tenure or retirement statute in which contractual status prevails under the law (*Ball v. Board of Trustees*, 1904). The clause also protects from arbitrary dismissal those school personnel who are employed under contract. A teacher who has a contract may be dismissed during the term of that contract only with showing of cause and due process. This article has been litigated in numerous public school cases.

First Amendment

First Amendment implications for education are developed in greater detail in a later chapter in this text. Only a brief discussion is presented here. The First Amendment addresses several basic personal freedoms. It provides that

> Congress shall make no law respecting an establishment of religion, or prohibiting the free exercise thereof; or abridging the freedom of speech, or of press; or the right of the people peaceably to assemble, and to petition the Government for a redress of grievances.

The Freedom of Religion Clause has become an honest—and sometimes dishonest—source of conflict in America's schools. Since the mid-20th century schools have become the battleground for some of the most volatile disputes over the appropriate role of religion in public life (McCarthy, Cambron-McCabe, & Thomas, 1998). In addition, the first part of the amendment, the phrase regarding religious freedom, has led to litigation challenging government aid to parochial schools.

The freedom of speech clause has resulted in numerous court cases involving rights of students and teachers to freedom of expression. Over the past several decades, student rights under this amendment have been extended to total freedom of speech on school grounds (Odden, 1995). Students and their attorneys have addressed situations ranging from demonstrations against governmental action to censorship of writings in student newspapers.

Another Constitutional issue is the degree to which students have fundamental rights as against the authority of school officials to restrict student behavior. The right of assembly section has precipitated litigation involving student organizations as well as employee rights to organize and bargain collectively.

Among the many court decisions based on the First Amendment are the following:

- Neither students nor teachers shed their Constitutional rights to freedom of speech or expression at the schoolhouse gate (*Tinker v. Des Moines*, 1969)

- School districts may develop dress codes and regulate hair length (*Massie v. Henry*, 1972)
- Lewd and indecent speech by students is not protected by the First Amendment (*Bethel School District No. 403 v. Fraser*, 1986).

Fourth Amendment

The Fourth Amendment provides that "the right of people to be secure in their persons, houses, papers, and effects, against unreasonable searches and seizures, shall not be violated, and no warrants shall issue, but upon probable cause." This amendment has been the subject of litigation involving searches of students' lockers and persons as well as teachers' rights to privacy.

The issues surrounding search and seizure of students have grown in complexity in recent years. Increasingly, schoolteachers and administrators are concerned with drug possession and use by students. This situation is not likely to abate in the next several years. Overall drug use has declined slightly since its peak in 1996-97, but it is still well above figures reported in 1991. Thus, in the year 2000 use of an illicit drug in the previous 30 days was reported by 24.9% of high school seniors, as compared with 16.4% in 1991. If marijuana is eliminated, the figure for 2000 declines to 10.4%. On the other hand, use of so dangerous a drug as Ecstasy by seniors has risen sharply, from 2.0% in 1996 (when first on the survey) to 3.6% in 2000. Similar rises in use of that drug are seen at the eighth- and tenth-grade levels (Johnston, O'Malley, & Bachman, 2000).

Weapons on campus have also greatly increased in the past decade. The Fourth Amendment, written to protect citizens against unreasonable search and seizure, has been interpreted as requiring law enforcement officials to have probable cause that a crime has been committed and to obtain a search warrant before conducting a search. Prior to 1985 some courts held school officials to the same standard. However, in *New Jersey v. T.L.O.* (1985), the U.S. Supreme Court ruled that school officials' interest in maintaining discipline in the schools was sufficient to justify a lesser standard than probable cause. Consequently, school officials may conduct searches based on a "reasonable suspicion" provided that:

- there is "individualized" reasonable cause or suspicion that the search will reveal evidence of a violation of the law or school rules, and

- the scope of the search is reasonably related to the objective of the search and is not "excessively intrusive" in light of the age and sex of the child and the nature of the alleged infraction.

In determining whether a particular search is reasonable, the courts have distinguished between school property, such as lockers, and personal property. The courts have decided that students may have exclusive use of a locker with regard to other students, but possession is not exclusive with regard to school officials, who retain control of the lockers. In fact, courts have said that it is the duty of school officials to search a locker if suspicion arises that something of an illegal nature may be concealed there (*People v. Overton*, 1969).

A topic of controversy at many school sites is use of drug-sniffing dogs to help eliminate the drug problem on campus. Courts disagree on this issue, too. In *Doe v. Renfrow* (1980) the Seventh Circuit Court viewed use of dogs as preliminary to the search itself and therefore legal, provided the dogs were used to detect a substance on particular students, not all students or random groups. An opposing conclusion was reached by the Fifth Circuit Court in *Horton v. Goose Creek Independent School District* (1982), which ruled that using drug-detecting dogs to sniff students is an unconstitutional invasion of student privacy. The Horton case did not preclude school officials from using dogs to search lockers and cars. Presumably, this conflict will be resolved at some point by the U.S. Supreme Court.

Strip searches of students have generally not been upheld to recover stolen items of minor significance (*Bellnier v. Land, 1977*). However, given the perceived extent of the drug problem among school-aged children, courts are granting increased latitude to school officials in conducting strip searches (*Cornfield v. Consolidated High School District No. 230*, 1993). These searches have generally been upheld by the courts where "reasonable suspicion was established by word of mouth among school employees and students, bulges in clothes, and other indications of concealment of drugs" (Alexander & Alexander, 2001).

Turning to employees' right to privacy, we note that litigation has arisen with regard to health and physical requirements for school employees, especially where testing is required for AIDS infection or for use of alcohol or drugs. The courts have held that mandatory urine and blood tests, if neither part of a routine medical examination required by law nor agreed to by the employee, violate the Fourth Amendment prohibition against unreasonable searches. However, such testing may be required in case of an "individualized 'reasonable' suspicion" of a condition that imperils the proper functioning of the employee or the well-being of others coupled with unavailability of any less intrusive means of resolving the suspicion (Valente, 1998). Should an employee's history or job duties affect student safety, the employer may require relevant testing without violating the Fourth Amendment. Bus drivers form the employee group that most commonly falls into this category.

Fifth Amendment

For schools, the pertinent part of the Fifth Amendment guarantees that "no person . . . shall be compelled in any criminal case to be a witness against himself, nor be deprived of life, liberty, or property, without due process of law; nor shall private property be taken for public use, without just compensation." The first clause is relevant to cases in which teachers have been questioned by supervisors about alleged activities with subversive organizations. In education cases, this clause has been invoked by teachers who refused to answer questions about their affiliations and activities outside of school. The courts have granted school officials the right to require employees to answer questions about their activities outside the classroom, but only if the activities relate to the teacher's qualifications or fitness to teach (*Beilan v. Board of Public Education*, 1958).

The due process protection of the Fifth Amendment is not usually cited in education cases because it pertains specifically to acts of the federal government. Rather, the Due Process Clause of the Fourteenth Amendment is used because it applies directly to the states.

The last clause in the Fifth Amendment is important in those cases where a state or school system is seeking to obtain private property for school purposes. This right of the government to take private property for the common good is called the "right of eminent domain." The right is exercised by a state or school district when an owner refuses to sell property for such purposes as a government building or a school site. When the power of eminent domain is exercised, the owner of the property must be given just compensation.

Eighth Amendment

The part of the Eighth Amendment that generally relates to schools is the section that provides protection against "cruel and unusual punishment." This amendment has been invoked to challenge corporal punishment in schools. The U.S. Supreme Court has decided that corporal punishment is not cruel and unusual punishment as anticipated by the Eighth Amendment (*Ingraham v. Wright*, 1977). However, this decision does not prohibit states or school districts from restricting such punishment. Thus, as discussed in another section of this text, corporal punishment is forbidden in California.

Tenth Amendment

As noted earlier, the Tenth Amendment to the U.S. Constitution provides: "The powers not delegated to the United States by the Constitution nor prohibited by it to the States, are reserved to the States respectively, or to the people." This clause confers on states the authority to control education and to devise and implement their own system of taxation. This state power to control education was tested in an early Supreme Court case (*U.S. v. Butler*, 1936), when the Court concluded that "all powers not expressly granted to the United States by the Constitution or reasonably implied therefrom were reserved to the states." This statement provided a case law basis for the power of a state to tax and to appropriate funds for public schools.

Fourteenth Amendment

The Fourteenth Amendment, approved in 1868 in the wake of the Civil War, is the Constitutional provision most often invoked in education-related cases because it pertains specifically to state actions. The Fourteenth Amendment provides that no state shall "deprive any person of life, liberty or property, without due process of law." Numerous education cases citing this provision have come to the courts. Liberty rights include interest in one's reputation and the right to personal privacy. Property rights include a tenured teacher's right to continued employment and a student's right, under compulsory school attendance laws, to attend school.

The Fourteenth Amendment also provides that no state shall "deny to any person within its jurisdiction the equal protection of the law." This Equal Protection Clause has been relied upon in a wide variety of education cases in recent years. Some cases have addressed alleged discrimination based on race, ethnic background, sex, age, or handicapping condition; others have dealt with inequity in state financing of public schools.

Bear in mind that the Fourteenth Amendment has been interpreted by the courts to require both substantive and procedural due process. The definition of substantive due process is vague, but is generally construed to involve the constitutionality of the content of the charges. Procedural due process is more definitively described and requires two conditions: notification and fair hearing. In numerous cases, the courts have made it clear that both types of due process must be present to suspend or expel a student (*Garcia by Garcia v. Miera*, 1987; *Goss v. Lopez*, 1975).

State Constitutions

The United States is organized into two divisions of government activity: a federal legal system and fifty separate state legal systems. Each state has its own constitution to establish its basic laws. Like the U.S. Constitution, state constitutions provide a foundation for enactment of innumerable statutes that govern the activities of the state and its citizens. However, unlike the federal Constitution, every state constitution includes a provision for education. These provisions range from very specific to very general. They have in common the overall intent to ensure that schools and education are encouraged and that a uniform system of schools is established (Webb, 1996).

The education section in each state constitution is very important to the courts in determining whether particular legislative enactments are Constitutionally required, permissible, or inappropriate. While state constitutions establish a framework for education, they do not give unlimited power to state legislatures in providing for the public schools. Rather, they set the boundaries within which each legislature may operate. Thus, a state legislature must act within the scope of both state and federal constitutions.

Collins (1969) reported that the constitutions of 45 states provided for the establishment of "common schools," and 35 states established specific methods for financial support. The constitutions of 30 states expressly prohibit use of public funds in religious schools, and the constitution of every state except Maine and North Carolina contains a provision prohibiting religious instruction in public schools.

The Constitution of California

Contrary to the U.S. Constitution that, as we have seen, does not mention education, California's first constitution, adopted in 1849, established the office of State Superintendent of Public Instruction. Following this action, other laws were passed regarding education (Kunzi, 1978). In 1879, California replaced the 1849 constitution with a new document. The new constitution was more specific and detailed than the earlier version. Although it has been amended many times, its basic structure and pattern remain unchanged (Palmer, 1983).

The importance of education was acknowledged in the 1879 constitution. A philosophy of education was expressed in Article IX, Section 1, of that constitution. This section requires the legislature to encourage intellectual, scientific, moral, and agricultural improvement:

> A general diffusion of knowledge and intelligence being essential to the preservation of the rights and liberties of the people, the Legislature shall encourage by all suitable means the promotion of intellectual, scientific, moral and agricultural improvement. The distribution and sale of published material, including copyright material, has been declared by the Legislature to be a public purpose in furtherance of Article IX, section 1.

Other sections of the 1879 constitution also address educational issues; it retained the State Superintendent of Public Instruction and included a state Board of Education, county superintendents of schools, and county boards of education. Other sections dealt with financial aid to schools, a minimum salary for teachers, and adoption of textbooks. The 1879 constitution also provided that no public money might be appropriated to support sectarian or denominational schools and that no sectarian or denominational doctrine could be taught in the public schools.

Almost from the day when the 1879 constitution was approved, dissatisfaction with it surfaced. The 1897 legislature considered a new Constitutional Convention, but 60% of the electorate rejected the idea. No further proposal was submitted to the people until 1913, when the legislature again raised to the electorate the question of a Constitutional Convention. This proposal, too, was soundly defeated.

Discussion of a complete revision of the 1879 California constitution has continued until the present. Over the years the constitution has become swollen with obsolete items and minutiae. By 1929 nearly 200 amendments had been approved. However, the next effort to revise the 1879 constitution did not occur until 1963. At that time the legislature created the California Constitution Revision Commission, a 60-member panel that included distinguished state leaders drawn from virtually every sector of the population. Some pruning of the constitution was clearly in order because the California constitution then contained more than 75,000 words; it was ten times the length of the U.S. Constitution and longer than any other state constitution except that of Louisiana.

The work of the 1963 commission was not completed until the election of June 1976. Suggested changes were submitted to the voters in 1966 and 1968. The 1966 election resulted in elimination of some 16,000 of the 22,000 words in selected sections. The 1968 proposals would have reduced the constitution from 14,000 words to 2,000, but this proposition was rejected by the voters. Through 1986, the California constitution had been amended 460 times, yet still another California Constitution Revision Commission was established in 1993.

Initiatives and Referenda

The initiative and referendum are products of a movement toward direct democracy that was led by the Progressive faction of the Republican Party around 1900. The initiative gives California citizens the right to propose statutes and amend the state constitution. California is one of the few states in which the initiative process may be used to amend the constitution—and the only one in which a statutory amendment adopted by initiative cannot be modified by the legislature unless the initiative so provides. Among the states that use the initiative process, California is by far the most active, and the initiative process has come increasingly to dominate the state's political culture.

Prior to 1966, the number of signatures required to place an initiative on the ballot was 8% of the total number of votes cast for gubernatorial candidates in the previous election. In 1966 the requirement was reduced to 5%. Obtaining signatures on petitions has become big business; firms hired by proponents to solicit signatures charge as much as $2 for each signature obtained. An initiative measure that obtains the required number of signatures is submitted to the voters at the next general election, unless the Governor calls for a special statewide election.

A referendum gives the electorate power to approve or reject statutes or parts of statutes. To be placed on the ballot, a referendum, like an initiative, requires signatures of 5% of the electorate. Passage of a referendum measure does not necessarily result in adoption of a law, but may operate to prevent a statute adopted by the legislature from having legal effect.

Federal Statutes

Every legislature enacts, amends, and repeals laws. These laws, or statutes, constitute the second highest level of law, following constitutions. Whereas constitutions provide broad statements of policy, statutes establish the specifics of operation. Both the U.S. Congress and state legislatures have passed innumerable laws that affect education.

During each legislative session the U.S. Congress enacts or renews numerous statutes that impact public schools. Many of these statutes provide financial assistance for a variety of special instructional programs, research, and services for needy children. Examples at the national level include Chapter 1, Economic Impact Aid, the food services program, and Native American education. Other examples of federal legislation that impact education include civil rights legislation, funds for vocational education, and rules and regulations regarding special education.

Federal statutes are subject to review by the federal courts, which determine whether a law violates the federal constitution. If not, it is binding on all citizens and governmental agencies. As we shall see, a similar relationship exists between state statutes and state courts; that is, state statutes are subject to challenge in state courts. In addition, state legislation and state court decisions, in those areas of responsibility not delegated to the states, must conform to federal law and the U.S. Constitution and may be subject to review in federal courts.

State Statutes

As previously discussed, although the Tenth Amendment grants to states the control of education, laws enacted by the states cannot override federal law or the state or federal constitution. Like Congress, successive state legislatures continually review and revise, supplement, repeal, and replace statutes.

Although delegating the actual operation of school districts to local boards, a state legislature also responds to societal needs and pressure groups by enacting new or revising old legislation. Some acts are general in nature and leave broad discretion to school boards, while other legislation mandates specific actions to local boards. In addition to providing direction to school districts for general operation of the schools, most state governments retain operation of certain types of specialized schools, such as those for the blind and deaf.

California Education Code

Nearly all California laws regarding education are published in the Education Code, although some provisions are also found in other codes, such as the Government Code. The Education Code is not based on a prior code, but is a collection of rules and regulations for the organization and administration of California's public schools. As the state has increased in population, the laws affecting education have increased in number and complexity. This collection of laws is contained in eleven volumes and is updated each year. It is also posted and searchable on the Internet at http://www.leginfo.ca.gov/calaw.html.

Administrators and attorneys who specialize in school law will verify that the statutes contained in the Education Code are complex, ambiguous, and often contradictory. Superintendents, often with a tone of humor and remorse, refer to the Education Code as "full employment for attorneys." To add credence to this view, California Supreme Court Justice Stanley Mosk made the following observation about the Education Code:

> Both parties agree that it i[illegible]oncile sections of the Education Code. Ap[illegible]ole is a crazy-quilt product of we[illegible]ccommodate the divergen[illegible] the public. To o[illegible], the result is like [illegible]inion in *Taylor v.*

[illegible]rnia joined the union in 1850 that the legisla[illegible]irst session of the legislature enacted a total of 146 chapters. [illegible]blished the structure of local government, formalized a system of taxat[illegible]regulated elections (Palmer, 1983). Over the next several decades numerou[illegible]laws were enacted. Keeping track of the various enactments became a complex and difficult task. Therefore, in 1929, the legislature created the California Code Commission. The Commission was given the task of codifying all of California's laws.

The Commission reviewed all the laws passed in previous sessions of the legislature and recommended creation of the Education Code (Kunzi, 1978). The Education Code was subsequently revised in 1959 and in 1977. These revisions did not result in substantive changes in the statutes, but were attempts to collect and codify statutes that had been enacted over the years.

In 1972 the people of California, through the initiative process, made a major change in the Education Code. This initiative changed the philosophy of the Education Code from a *mandatory* to a *permissive code.* Prior to this change in the state constitution, school districts were seen as agencies of the state with limited authority. Responding to the initiative, the legislature enacted Education Code Sections 35160 (applicable to elementary and secondary districts) and 70902 (applicable to community colleges), which are virtually identical. Education Code Section 35160 states:

> On and after January 1, 1976, the governing board of any school district may initiate and carry on any program, activity, or may otherwise act in any manner which is not in conflict with or inconsistent with, or preempted by, any law and which is not in conflict with the purposes for which school districts are established.

In theory, the approval of this initiative by the citizens of California grants school districts greater latitude to make decisions at the school district level. In practice, many of the restrictions of the Education Code are still in place and require a district to seek legal advice prior to establishing a new regulation or procedure. Port (1998) states that the failure of the legislature to revise the code to accommodate its new permissiveness has resulted in confusion and, consequently, the permissive language is of little value.

Most school boards and superintendents still feel restricted by the mandates of the Education Code and lobby to have it abolished completely. Nevertheless, some—perhaps those who were bolder or more creative—state that they are no longer required to lobby legislators for approval of a new program and claim greater latitude in local decision-making.

Title V—Administrative Code

In addition to confusion over the requirements of the Education Code, Title V of the California Code of Regulations, which contains the rules and regulations established by the California Department of Education to implement the Education Code, often interprets code sections in ways that are conflicting and difficult to understand. Also, as a result of the large number of education laws approved each year, Title V has not been kept up-to-date.

In lieu of keeping Title V current, the California Department of Education attempts to interpret legislation and provide direction by sending advisory letters to school districts. This advice is often frustrating to school administrators. For example, Assembly Bill 3482 was approved by the legislature and signed by the Governor in 1996. This legislation established a program known as the "Teacher Reading Instruction Development Program." One section of the bill requires

> that each certificated teacher of pupils enrolled in kindergarten and grades 1 to 3, inclusive, possess the knowledge and skills to effectively teach pupils to read.

Sounds quite clear cut, right? However, the advisory letter from Ruth McKenna (1996), Chief Deputy Superintendent, addressed to all district and county superintendents, reads:

> The district agrees to provide certification to the California Department of Education on or before August 30, 1997, that not less than 90 percent of certificated employees who provide direct instructional services to pupils enrolled in kindergarten or any of the

grades 1 to 3, inclusive, have received inservice training in the reading components.

The letter from McKenna included a place for the school superintendent to certify that the training had been accomplished. If you were a school superintendent, required to provide the training and certify that it had been accomplished, would you be clear as to who had to be trained? The law reads, "kindergarten and grades 1 to 3, inclusive." The Department of Education directive states, "kindergarten or any of the grades 1 to 3, inclusive." Must you train all kindergarten, first-, second-, and third-grade teachers? Or might you use the word "any" in the directive from McKenna and only train teachers in kindergarten and *either* grade one, two, *or* three? One school superintendent and her staff spent valuable time attempting to interpret the directive, called the county superintendent of schools, and were still uncertain about their obligations.

Other California Codes

In addition to the Education Code, California has several other collections of statutes organized by topic, among them the Government Code, Welfare and Institutions Code, Penal Code, Public Contracts Code, Business and Professions Code, and the Health and Safety Code. Each of these codes contains sections that directly affect education.

For example, the Public Contracts Code contains regulations regarding the awarding of contracts for school construction. The Health and Safety Code gives direction to the school nutrition program. The Government Code describes procedures for conducting "closed sessions" at school board meetings. As one would expect, a number of statutes affecting school discipline are contained in the Penal Code, including a section (628.2) that requires each school principal, at specified intervals, to submit to the superintendent a complete report of crimes committed on school grounds.

The Court System

The provisions of federal and state constitutions, statutes, and policies of local boards of education do not guarantee proper execution of the law. The founding fathers developed a three-prong system of government: the legislative branch to make the law, the executive branch to enforce the law, and the courts to interpret the law.

The court system provides a means through which individuals or groups who believe their constitutional rights have been violated may seek adjudication. It is important to remember that the courts do not take action on their own initiative. Rather, it is the role of the judiciary to resolve disputes by interpreting a law after its enactment and to review its constitutionality. Courts settle only those disputes referred to them for a decision (Reutter, 1994). In school-related matters, the courts have generally taken the position that they will not intervene in a dispute unless all internal appeals—that is, appeals within the district, county, and state education structure—have been reviewed and exhausted (Webb, 1996).

Nevertheless, despite their solely reactive mode, courts have limited the authority of government over public education at both federal and state levels as school operations have been challenged in the courts. Decisions on issues ranging from corporal punishment to racial desegregation of public schools have been made by the courts. On the other hand, courts have affirmed the authority of states to regulate such matters as certification, powers of school boards, curriculum requirements, the school calendar, accreditation, and numerous financial matters.

Federal Judicial System

An action involving a federal issue may be filed in a federal district court. Issues that qualify for hearing at the federal level include civil rights, free speech, due process, and equal protection. Once a lawsuit is filed in a particular court system, that system retains jurisdiction until conclusion of the issue. For example, a case on appeal from a federal district court goes to the federal court of appeals for the circuit in which that federal district court is located.

California is in the Ninth Circuit. The Ninth Circuit includes Alaska, Washington, Oregon, Hawaii, Arizona, Nevada, Idaho, Montana, Northern Mariana Islands, California, and Guam. Cases brought in the federal courts in any of these states or territories may be appealed to the federal Court of Appeals for the Ninth Circuit. Circuit court decisions are binding throughout the circuit in which they are rendered. If a plaintiff is dissatisfied with the decision of the federal court of appeals, a further appeal may be made to the U.S. Supreme Court. However, the Supreme Court is not required to consider an appeal, but must agree to hear the matter. This agreement is referred to as "certiorari," abbreviated "cert." This procedure is used by the Supreme Court as a discretionary device to choose the cases it wishes to hear.

The U.S. Supreme Court is the court of final appeal on federal law questions. Of the education-related questions that eventually reach the court, petitioners most frequently claim that a state's statutes or the policies of a local board of education have violated their Constitutional rights or some provision of federal law. As discussed in later sections of this text, the U.S. Supreme Court has made numerous decisions regarding education. For example, corporal punishment, affirmative action, sex discrimination, compulsory attendance, and school-church issues have been considered by the Court.

Thousands of cases are appealed to the Supreme Court each year, with only a small number being heard. However, in recent years the number of education cases appealed to and heard by the Supreme Court has increased. This trend of parents and citizens to sue in the courts accelerated markedly after the *Brown v. Board of Education* decision in 1954. Once segregation had been declared unconstitutional, other educational policies were challenged in the courts. Examples include prayer in the schools, government aid to parochial schools, compulsory school attendance, education of the handicapped, and student discipline (Wenkart, 1995).

State Judicial System

There are two types of courts in California: trial courts and courts of appeal, the latter including the California Supreme Court. Formerly, municipal (urban) and justice (rural) courts constituted a level of trial court below the superior courts. However, in 54 of the state's 58 counties, all trial courts have unified into a single superior court in response to Proposition 220, passed in 1998. Included within the trial court structure are several specialized courts: small claims courts (for issues that do not exceed $5,000), family and juvenile courts, traffic courts, and criminal courts (Judicial Council, 2001).

Most actions involving school districts originate in the superior court of the county in which the district is located. The most common action used by a plaintiff in an action against a school district is a petition for a writ of mandate (Port, 1998). This action is a request for a court order requiring a school district to take, or refrain from taking, a particular action.

Appeals from superior court decisions proceed to the courts of appeal in the judicial district in which the superior court is located. If the plaintiff appeals the decision of a court of appeal, the matter goes to the California Supreme Court. Like the U.S. Supreme Court, the California Supreme Court is not required to hear a matter and may let the decision stand as decided by the court of appeal.

Complexity of the Court System

The complexity of California's court system, and its interaction with the legislature and Governor may be illustrated by the 1991 bankruptcy of Richmond Unified, since renamed to the West Contra Costa County Unified, School District. Actions are listed chronologically in Table 1. These circumstances were reported in the *Los Angeles Times* (LAT), *Oakland Tribune* (OT), *Sacramento Bee* (SB), *San Francisco Business Times* (SFBT), *San Francisco Chronicle* (SFC), and *San Francisco Examiner* (SFE) on the dates indicated. Among the chief actors in this drama were Governor Wilson, State Superintendent of Public Instruction Bill Honig, and Controller Gray Davis. One can observe that cases were brought in Small Claims Court (at that time a part of the municipal court), Superior Court, the California Supreme Court, the U.S. Bankruptcy Court, and the U.S. District Court. Also involved were the state legislature, the Contra Costa County Grand Jury, and the district's insurance carrier. It should be noted that in the wake of the bankruptcy, legislation was passed giving county superintendents of schools oversight of district finances and the state authorization to take over an insolvent district, as is discussed further in chapter 10.

Case Law

Case law differs from statutes, regulations, or other sources of law in that it consists of that body of law originating from historical usage and custom and from previous court decisions. When conflict occurs regarding the interpretation of a law, courts resolve these conflicts; such decisions become known as case law. Case law is based on the doctrine of *stare decisis*, which means "let the decision stand." The doctrine requires that once a court has laid down a principle of law as applicable to a certain set of facts, it will apply that principle to all future cases in which the facts are substantially the same. Other courts of equal or lesser rank will apply the principle similarly (*Black's*, 1999).

The doctrine of case law does not mean that previous decisions are never challenged or overturned. A higher or subsequent court may reject the reasoning of a lower or earlier court and overturn a previous decision. A court may even reverse its own prior decision. Perhaps the most notable example of the U.S. Supreme Court reversing itself on reconsideration is the case of *Brown v. Board of Education of Topeka* (1954). In *Plessy v. Ferguson* (1896) the Supreme Court had said "separate but equal" schools for blacks and whites were Constitutionally permissible. The *Brown* decision reversed this position and ruled that separate schools for blacks and whites were inherently unequal, hence unconstitutional.

Table 1.
Richmond Unified School District and the Courts

Date	Action	News-paper
6-8-90	RUSD reported a $9 million deficit.	SFC
2-19-91	RUSD announced it was considering filing for bankruptcy.	SFC
4-18-91	RUSD board voted unanimously to file for bankruptcy. California Teachers Association filed suit in Superior Court to force the state to provide bailout funds. Parents filed in Superior Court (class action suit) for an injunction to prevent the schools from closing on May 1.	SFC, SB, OT
4-20-91	RUSD filed for bankruptcy in U.S. Bankruptcy Court, the first California district to do so.	SFC
4-29-91	Disability Rights Education Defense Fund, Inc. (DREDF) filed in U.S. District Court in Sacramento for a restraining order to prevent schools from closing six weeks early.	SFC
4-30-91	Superior Court judge ordered the state and the State Superintendent of Public Instruction to find funds to keep RUSD schools open. U.S. District Court judge refused to grant temporary restraining order sought by DREDF, but scheduled June 5 hearing on a mandatory injunction.	SFC, OT
5-1-91	The State Controller and State Superintendent devised a $19 million loan to RUSD, but the Governor said he would appeal to overthrow the ruling of the Superior Court.	SFE
5-3-91	Superior Court judge approved the $19 million loan and ordered RUSD to remain open. In place of the school board, a trustee was to run the district for five years under the State Superintendent. Collective bargaining was to be resumed with the state in the place of the district; a court-approved settlement would prevail if agreement were not reached by July 7. The union reserved its right to strike.	SFC, SFE
5-10-91	The state appealed the Superior Court order to the California Supreme Court.	SFBT
6-4-91	The Contra Costa County grand jury found that the RUSD board (not the former superintendent) was responsible for bankruptcy by spending 26% above revenues.	SFC

Table 1.
Richmond Unified School District and the Courts (cont'd)

Date	Action	News-paper
7-17-91	A parent committee asked for a voice in proceedings in U.S. Bankruptcy Court.	SFC
8-27-91	RUSD filed with U.S. Bankruptcy Court a request to discontinue bankruptcy proceedings.	SB
9-25-91	Representatives of RUSD teachers, parents, and clerical employees announced opposition to dismissing the bankruptcy proceedings.	SFC
10-4-91	U.S. Bankruptcy Court judge announced that RUSD bankruptcy had to be dismissed because bankruptcy is a voluntary action. Newspaper stated debts had risen to "at least $54 million," staff had been dismissed, and RUSD had reduced teachers' salaries by 9% and the school day to five periods.	SFC
1-23-92	RUSD projected a $2.1 million deficit for 1992-93.	SFC
2-13-92	State Superintendent filed a $28.5 million claim with the self-insurance pool for state schools, claiming that RUSD had misused funds and neglected its duty and asking that the sum be placed in a fund to relieve the district of its debt. The Governor objected.	SFC
7-23-92	In April two parents had filed $5,000 suits in Small Claims Court against the State Superintendent and RUSD state trustee, claiming their children had received an inferior education; cases were to be heard on July 23. (The outcome was not reported in the press.)	SFC
9-2-92	Legislature passed a bill to wipe out RUSD's $29 million debt	SFC
10-2-92	Governor vetoed the debt bail-out. The earlier insurance claim having been denied as filed too late, State Superintendent sued RUSD in Superior Court for $58.5 million, hoping to recover from the district's insurance carrier. Governor said such a suit "was not unprecedented."	SFC
1-1-93	California Supreme Court decided unanimously that state has a constitutional duty to intervene in insolvency to ensure basic education for all pupils, including a 175-day school year, but 4-3 determined that a judge could not order the state to provide money unless the legislature had appropriated it. The court did not, however, rescind the state loan.	LAT, SFC, SB

Administrative Law

Administrative law consists of the formal regulations and decisions of state and federal agencies that govern public functions. These regulations carry the force of law. They are subject to judicial review and stand as law unless found to conflict with federal or state constitutional provisions, statutes, or applicable case law.

At the federal level, the U.S. Department of Education and the National Institute of Education are the agencies most directly concerned with education. The director of each of these departments is appointed by the President. Other federal agencies that establish regulations affecting education include the Department of Agriculture, the Department of the Interior, the Bureau of Indian Affairs, and the Department of Labor.

In California, the state agencies that have most control over education are the California Department of Education and the state Board of Education. The members of the California Board of Education are appointed by the Governor, with the advice and consent of the state senate, while the State Superintendent of Instruction is elected by the people. Generally, after the legislature has enacted a law, the California Department of Education is responsible for issuing a regulation to guide local districts in implementing the law. These regulations can affect almost every aspect of school operations, including adoption of textbooks, bilingual education, and certification of teachers.

Attorney General Opinions

Another source of education law is the official opinions of the state attorney general. The attorney general is the chief legal officer of the state and acts as legal advisor to state agencies. Often, the attorney general is requested to render an opinion regarding interpretation of a law. This request usually originates with the Governor, a legislator, or a local official. While such opinions are advisory, they are helpful in clarifying and interpreting the law (LaMorte, 1999).

Access to Legal Information

Many United States and California court cases, California Department of Education policies and guidelines, the Education Code, and associated information are available via the Internet. Access may be obtained through search engines such as

Google (http://www.google.com). A comprehensive list of Internet search engines is maintained at the All-in-One Search Page (http://www.AllOneSearch.com).

Information, especially about legal resources, is also accessible through the homepages of Kenneth Lane, Professor at California State University, San Bernardino (http://dcr.csusb.edu/soe/klane/ and click on "Links") and John Burton, Director of Student Services, Fontana Unified School District, (http://www.fontana.k12.ca.us/burton/). The California constitution, all California codes, including the Education Code and the Government Code, and current bills may be accessed at http://www.leginfo.ca.gov/. A list of Internet resources on the law is provided in chapter 2, Table 2. Finally, California counties maintain law libraries that are open to the public.

Summary

American public schools are governed by a complex body of directives derived from constitutional provisions, statutory enactments, agency regulations, and court decisions. The sources of law include many different agencies within both the state of California and the federal government. In addition, the courts, through their decisions on the multitude of cases they hear, provide direction in interpreting policies enacted by the California legislature and the Congress of the United States.

Education law cannot be interpreted on the basis of one agency or one policy. All policies and agencies must be considered in understanding and applying the sources of law. While educators are not required to have formal legal training, they must be aware of the many facets of laws that govern day-to-day management of schools. School personnel, like any citizen, cannot plead ignorance of the law as a defense for illegal actions. Educators must be knowledgeable of school board policies and keep current on changing legislation and court decisions that affect their school leadership.

Key Terms

1. attorney general opinions
2. case law
3. Education Code
4. Eighth Amendment
5. federal judicial system
6. federal statutes
7. First Amendment
8. Fourth Amendment
9. Fifth Amendment
10. Tenth Amendment
11. Fourteenth Amendment
12. General Welfare Clause
13. initiative
14. Obligation of Contracts Clause
15. permissive education code
16. referendum
17. right of eminent domain
18. *stare decisis*
19. state statutes
20. state judicial system
21. Title V—Administrative Code

Discussion / Essay Questions

1. It may seem strange to modern Americans that the founding fathers did not mention education in the U.S. Constitution. Was this just an oversight, or was there a reason for its absence?

2. The courts have generally upheld the power of Congress to pass legislation that collects taxes and spends monies for education. What section of the federal Constitution is cited to support this decision? What are the grounds for the decision?

3. *New Jersey v. T.L.O.* greatly clarified discipline on school campuses. Give a brief review of this decision. Discuss how it clarified the ability of school administrators to maintain discipline.

4. The California constitution generally maintains the structure and pattern that were established when it was approved in 1879. What are the arguments pro and con for a complete revision of the 1879 constitution?

5. Most of California's laws affecting education are included in the Education Code. This code is referred to as a "permissive" code. What does that term mean? Has the idea been useful to California educators?

References

Alexander, K., & Alexander, M. D. (2001). *American public school law* (5th ed.). Belmont, CA: West/Thomson Learning.

Black's Law Dictionary (7th ed.). (1999). Bryan A. Garner, Editor-in-Chief. St. Paul, MN: West Group.

Collins, G. J. (1969). Constitutional and legal basis for state action. In E. Fuller & J. B. Pearson (Eds.), *Education in the states: Nationwide development since 1900.* Washington, DC: National Education Association.

Johnston, L. D., O'Malley, P. M., & Bachman, J. G. (2000, December). "Ecstasy" use rises sharply among teens in 2000; use of many other drugs steady, but significant declines are reported for some. Ann Arbor, MI: University of Michigan News and Information Services. Retrieved Dec. 29, 2000, from the World Wide Web: http://www.monitoringthefuture.org/data/00data.htm

Judicial Council of California (2001). Guide to California Courts. Retrieved May 14, 2001, from the World Wide Web: http://www.courtinfo.ca.gov/

Kunzi, E. H. (1978). *The California Education Code.* St. Paul, MN: West.

LaMorte, M. W. (1999). *School law: Cases and concepts* (6th ed.). Boston: Allyn and Bacon.

McCarthy, M. M., Cambron-McCabe, N. H., & Thomas, S. B. (1998). *Public school law: Teachers' and students' rights* (4th ed.). Boston: Allyn & Bacon.

McKenna, R. (1996, September 5). New funds for reading professional development. Sacramento, CA: California Department of Education Advisory Letter.

Odden, A. R. (1995). *Educational leadership for America's schools.* New York: McGraw-Hill.

Palmer, W. J. (1983). *The development of law in California.* St. Paul, MN: West.

Port, L. (1998). *Between a rock and a hard place.* Foster City, CA: California School Law Publishers.

Reutter, E. E. (1994). *The law of public education* (4th ed.). Mineola, NY: Foundation Press.

Valente, W. D. (1998). *Law in the schools* (4th ed.). New York: Merrill.

Webb, L. D., Metha, A., & Jordan, K. F. (1996). *Foundations of American education* (2nd ed.). Englewood Cliffs, N.J.: Prentice Hall.

Wenkart, R. D. (1995). *The California educators' guide to school law* (2nd ed.). Costa Mesa, CA: Orange County Department of Education.

Court Cases

Ball v. Board of Trustees of Teachers Retirement Fund, 58 Atl. 111 (N.J. 1904)

Beilan v. Board of Education, School District of Philadelphia, 357 U.S. 399, 78 S.Ct. 1317 (1958)

Bellnier v. Land, 438 F.Supp. 47 (N.D.N.Y. 1977)

Bethel School District No. 403 v. Fraser, 478 U.S. 675, 106 S.Ct. 3159 (1986)

Brown v. Board of Education of Topeka, 347 U.S. 483 (1954)

Cornfield v. Consolidated High School District No. 230, 991 F.2d 1316 (7th Cir. 1993)

Doe v. Renfrow, 631 F.2d 91 (7th Cir. 1980)

Garcia by Garcia v. Miera, 817 F.2d 650 (10th Cir.1987)

Gibbons v. Ogden, 22 U.S. (9 Wheat) 1 (1824)

Goss v. Lopez, 419 U.S. 565, 95 S.Ct. 729 (1975)

Helvering v. Davis, 301 U.S. 619, 57 S.Ct. 904 (1937)

Horton v. Goose Creek Independent School District, 690 F.2d 470 (5th Cir. 1982)

Ingraham v. Wright, 430 U.S. 651 (1977)

Massie v. Henry, 455 F.2d 779 (4th Cir. 1972)

New Jersey, Petitioner v. T.L.O., 105 S.Ct. 733 (1985)

People v. Overton, 249 N.E. 2d 366 (N.Y. 1969)

Plessy v. Ferguson, 16 S.Ct. 1138 (1896)

Taylor v. Board of Trustees, 36 Cal.3d 500, 501 (1984)

Tinker v. Des Moines Independent Community School District, 393 U.S. 503, 89 S.Ct. 733 (1969)

U.S. v. Butler, 297 U.S. 1, 56 S.Ct. 312 (1936)

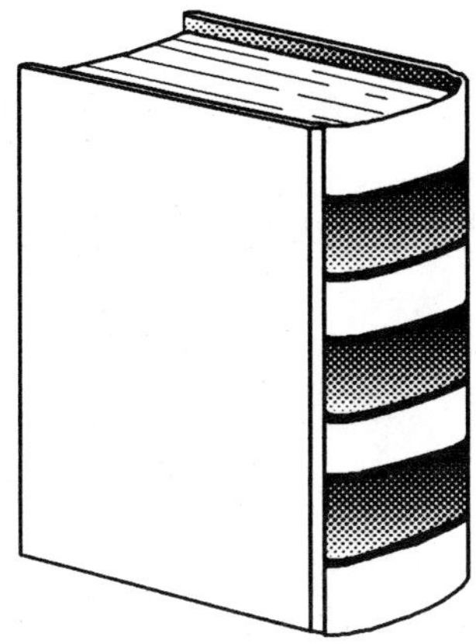

Chapter 2

Conducting Legal Research

Introduction

Legal research involves finding statutes, regulations, law cases, law reviews, and legal interpretations. These enable us to discuss intelligently the application of legal concepts to our job settings and everyday lives. Yell (1998) addresses this concept well:

> By accessing the law through legal research, educators will have a better understanding of the principles of law, the facts giving rise to these principles, and the application of those facts to situations they may encounter.

Research on legal issues is conducted in either of two basic ways. In the first instance, research may be conducted in a law library maintained at a university or in one of the public law libraries maintained by each county. The second way, which is growing in popularity, is via the Internet. Whichever option is chosen, certain principles must be followed.

As a beginning, primary legal documents and law-related commentaries are plentiful in both the physical and virtual law libraries. United States federal statutes, pending legislation and regulations, current federal appellate cases, California court opinions, legal opinions, and other information may be found. However, to conduct a successful search, the researcher must ask such questions as:

- Where does all this wonderful information reside?
- How do researchers determine when to scout the Web for information and when to rely on traditional resources?

- Do conventional online searching methods work at popular Web search sites?
- What other strategies should researchers apply?
- What evaluation skills should Internet researchers possess?

Furthermore, after finding the answer to a particular question, researchers must consider whether they can trust the information they find. To this end, questions must be raised to evaluate the quality and accuracy of any legal information. These questions include:

- Who is responsible for providing the information?
- Is it accurate, authentic, and complete?
- Is it timely and up-to-date?
- Is it objective?

And to use legal materials professionally, one must observe the usual guidelines regarding acknowledgment of sources, including the appropriate citation format for legal documents, whether obtained in print or via the Internet.

Information Access

West Group (2000) addresses the impact of information on those who conduct legal research when it states:

> The legal and information industries are going through some dramatic changes. Anticipating these changes, and recognizing the issues they raise for legal and business professionals, West Online has set in motion plans for the future that will enable us to adapt to the customer's evolving needs.
>
> Today, for example, there is an increased emphasis on specialization. Customers are demanding information tailored to their own specialties and jurisdictions. And, with the globalization of economies, the need for legal information internationally is critical for attorneys and business professionals alike. Complicating matters is the fact that traditional boundaries of information needs are changing. Law firms can no longer operate using only "legal" information, while businesses need access to more and more legal information in order to operate within the law and to maintain a diverse and changing labor

force. These professionals may need business news and information one day; public records the next; and regulatory, tax, or topical information the next. The need to put all of that information into the context of their situation requires tools that will enable them to cut through the myriad of content types and zero in on pertinent information.

Finally, domestic and international law is becoming more voluminous and complex, driving professionals' demand for easier ways to find and apply the law to any given situation. The ideal research products will point users to the right information and allow them to filter and make sense out of vast legal and nonlegal content in the easiest, most cost- and time-efficient manners.

Primary and Secondary Sources

Primary Sources

Before addressing research using a law library and the Internet, it may be helpful to discuss how information related to legal issues is defined as either a primary or secondary source. Primary sources are listed in chronological order, rather than by subject area. Examples of primary sources include federal and state statutes and regulations, as well as judicial decisions. Annotated codes, West's digest system, and Shepard's *Citations for Cases* are used to locate this primary material.

It should be noted that names of plaintiff and defendant sometimes reverse on appeal. Thus, if Smith sues the school district, the trial court case is identified as *Smith* [plaintiff] *v. Somewhere School District* [defendant]. If the school district loses and appeals, the new case may be named *Somewhere School District v. Smith*. In this situation, *Somewhere School District* becomes the appellant, and *Smith* is the respondent.

Federal statutes are organized by topic and published in a series of volumes called the United States Code (U.S.C.). There are 50 numbered titles in the U.S.C. The titles are divided into chapters and sections. Each title contains statutes covering a specific subject. The U.S.C. is considered the official version of federal statutes.

Annotated versions of the U.S.C. present information that is more useful than the text of the statute alone and are updated more frequently than the U.S.C. itself. There are two annotated versions—the United States Code Annotated (U.S.C.A.) and the United States Code Service (U.S.C.S.). These annotated editions contain information pertaining to each statute. The U.S.C.A. includes summaries of court cases that have interpreted each statute, notes and citations about the legislative history of the statute, cross-references to related statutes, and research guides to other relevant materials published by West. The U.S.C.S. reprints the statutes and, at the end of every section, examines relevant cases, provides citations to administrative materials, and lists other aids. It must be noted that the annotated codes contain updates in paper supplements that are filed in a pocket inside the back cover of each volume. A legal researcher must check these updates to determine whether a statute has recently been amended or even completely abolished.

One of the best ways to find a federal statute is through the citation that identifies its location. Citations are written in standard form—title, number, United States Code, section number followed by the subsection letter and number. An alternative way to find a federal statute is to use the Popular Name Index found at the end of the annotated codes. The index lists the popular name, statute number, date of passage, title, and section number. A third way to find a federal statute is to use the annotated code index, located at the back of the last volume, that lists statutes by subject.

Regulations are issued by administrative agencies to implement legislation. Federal regulations are published in the *Federal Register* and the *Code of Federal Regulations* (C.F.R.). The C.F.R. is organized by subject and contains 50 titles, each covering a general subject area. The C.F.R. contains the text of the regulation, a reference to the statute that authorizes the regulation, and the date of publication in the *Federal Register*.

As with federal statutes, one of the best ways to find a federal regulation is through the citation that identifies its location. The form for the citation is the same as in federal statutes—title, number, United States Code, section number followed by the subsection letter and number. An alternative way to find a federal regulation is to use the subject index at the end of each title of the C.F.R.

Law cases are published in volumes that are organized for federal courts according to the level of the court in which the case was decided, and for state courts, by geographical region and the level of the court. These volumes, called "reporters," are available in all law libraries. Sometimes, with diligent searching, a case may be found at a judicial site on the Internet.

The federal government does not publish the decisions of the federal district or appellate courts. The text of these decisions may be found in either of two ways—through Internet links or through the law reporters of the West Publishing Company. West publishes the decisions of the U.S. District Courts in the *Federal Supplement* (abbreviated F.Supp.). Decisions of the U.S. Courts of Appeals are published in the *Federal Reporter*. Internet links to the U.S. Courts of Appeal may be found on the Web homepage for Dr. Kenneth Lane, located at http://dcr.csusb.edu/soe/klane/.

The decisions of the U.S. Supreme Court are found in three different publications. *United States Supreme Court Reports* (abbreviated U.S.) is the official reporter because it is printed by the U.S. government. West publishes the *Supreme Court Reporter* (abbreviated S.Ct.). Bancroft-Whitney/Lawyers' Cooperative publishes the *Supreme Court Reports, Lawyers' Edition* (abbreviated L.Ed.). The latter two publications contain synopses, related cases, and historical information. Decisions of the California appellate courts, including the appeals and supreme courts, may be found in West's *California Reporter*.

State law cases are organized chronologically, rather than by subject. To help researchers find a state law case in any of the reporters, each published case includes a citation that follows a standard format. The format contains, in sequence, the name of the case, the volume number of the reporter, the title of the reporter, the page number followed by the court hearing the case, and the year in which the decision was rendered.

Secondary Sources

Secondary sources analyze or discuss legal doctrines and principles, but are not official because they are not actual statements of the law, merely interpretations of or opinions about the law. Nevertheless, they do tend to carry persuasive authority. Examples of secondary sources include legal journals such as West's *Education Law Reporter*, the *Journal of Law and Education*, and the Education Law Association's *Legal Notes* and *School Law Reporter*.

In addition, most law schools publish, either quarterly or annually, a law review that contains information on legal issues, historical research, and empirical studies. Typically, the law reviews contain articles written by legal scholars, commentary on legal issues, and book reviews.

Finally, there are newsletters published on a regular basis to address current issues in the legal field. Discussion of a legal issue in these newsletters is usually brief, but amplified with citations that direct the reader to more detailed information.

Bear in mind that there is always a sizeable time delay between the court decision and appearance of that decision in hard copy. Thus, Internet links provide the fastest access to the text of a recent court decision.

Using a Law Library

A law library contains the legal resources necessary to locate an actual law case. In California, every county maintains a law library for use by the public. For instance, in San Bernardino County, there are law libraries in San Bernardino and Rancho Cucamonga. In Riverside County, there are law libraries in Riverside and Indio.

Upon entering these law libraries, individuals may search the law volumes on their own or contact the librarian at the information or reference desk. One explains simply and briefly just what he or she is seeking, and the librarian will help find the necessary information. It has been the experience of both students and the authors that librarians' willingness to help makes a law library a comfortable place. Even those who generally use the Internet will find a visit to a law library an enriching educational experience.

Since most material cannot be checked out, patrons of a law library must be prepared to write the information they find on a legal pad or to photocopy it. A single copy of a limited quantity of material for nonprofit or scholarly purposes is generally considered fair use (see chapter 11). One may check with a librarian in case of concern about possible violation of copyright law.

Using the Internet

The Internet and the World Wide Web (commonly abbreviated WWW) are not the same thing; rather, the WWW is but one way to access material on the Internet. Nevertheless, the Web has nearly monopolized the practice of online research since it came into widespread use in 1995. Actually, the WWW is a collection of servers, all linked together via the Internet and all "speaking" a common computer language called "hypertext transmission protocol" (HTTP). These servers are accessible to client computers running browser software such as Netscape Navigator or Internet Explorer. Browser software communicates with the server using HTTP and receives and formats documents encoded in "hypertext mark-up language" (HTML).

Thus, The Internet is a network of networks, the physical collective of computers and wiring. The Internet can exist without the Web; however, the Web cannot exist without the Internet. HTTP, the protocol that allows Web servers and clients to talk to one another, is only one of several message protocols used on the

Internet. Others include e-mail (SMTP), newsgroups (NNTP), terminal emulation (Telnet), and file transfer protocol (FTP) (Chapman, 2000).

Generally, to use the World Wide Web one must have a computer with a Macintosh or Windows platform. Individual users access the Internet with a modem and telephone line (56K recommended), a cable modem from a cable television company, or other cable or wireless connection. Such services are available for a relatively low monthly subscription rate. Once connected to the Internet, the searcher enters the address (URL) of the desired server location, or "Website." (See Table 2 for a list of useful URLs.) Depending upon your browser's idiosyncrasies, http:// may or may not be needed in front of the Internet address.

Once connected to a useful Website, one sorts through the menus much as one might search a library catalog. If a searcher does not have a particular Website in mind, any one of several WWW search engines or lists of sources, sometimes called "Webliographies," will help locate information.

Two well-known sources for legal research on the Internet are LEXIS/NEXIS and Westlaw. Both require a subscription to use their services. Their addresses are:

LEXIS/NEXIS:	www.lexis.com
Westlaw:	www.westlaw.com

Numerous free Websites for research are also available. It must be noted that these Websites are only valuable and useful if the site is consistently and frequently maintained by someone with legal experience. Most of the sites shown in Table 2 are selected from the homepage of Dr. Kenneth E. Lane, posted at California State University, San Bernardino (http://dcr.csusb.edu/soe/klane/). Once there, click on "Links." It is important to note that Websites sometimes change their addresses. Therefore, additional searches may be needed.

A useful browser tool called "bookmarks" or "favorites" allows a searcher to keep a record of useful Internet locations. The bookmark can be recorded by the browser while the client computer is connected to the Website. Either menu items or keyboard commands (for example, Ctrl + D in Netscape Navigator) instruct the computer to bookmark the location. Thus, the list of bookmarks is essentially an address book or directory of Internet sites to which one can return merely by selecting the bookmark. The popular browsers keep a list of sites recently visited. Unfortunately, when the session ends, the list will be erased. It is, therefore, important to use the bookmark feature as the search is conducted.

Tips for Conducting a Law Search

The Virtual Chase Website (Ballard et al., 1999) at http://www.virtualchase.com/ provides these tips for using your browser to search for information.

> Researchers depending primarily on popular search engines to locate information likely will miss mounds of valuable resources. Why? Because search engines do not, arguably cannot, collect and index all data available on the Web. One recent updated analysis of the authors' earlier article appearing in *Science Magazine*, found that the Web houses an estimated 800 million pages, or six terabytes of text excluding coding. Yet search engines index a mere 16%, at best. . . . Clearly researchers must develop other strategies for discovering information.
>
> Consider how to research the issue in question without a computer, and then transfer the technique to the Internet. When seeking resources in a physical library, patrons typically check the card catalog, ask a librarian, or browse the shelves. Apply these techniques to the Web. Examples of catalogs include FindLaw and CataLaw. Look for discussion groups frequented by librarians using tools like DejaNews, Liszt, or CataList. Visit known and trusted sites to browse for related resources.
>
> To find federal government Websites, use Google: U.S. Government Search or Louisiana State University's U.S. Government Agencies Directory. To locate a state or local government site, try State and Local Government on the Net.

However, it is essential to know the source of information. Ballard et al. (1999) warn not to rely on information until its source, accuracy, authenticity, timeliness, and objectivity have been ascertained. Skepticism is a virtue on the Web. A checklist available on The Virtual Chase (see URL above) enables a searcher to evaluate the quality of information. Then, when a reliable source is found, the best advice is: "Don't let it go!" Reliable resources should be recorded with bookmarks, bookmark utilities, contact lists, card files, or one's own hyperlinked Web page.

Maximum benefit from the Internet is gained by focusing on those sites that are beneficial, not merely interesting. Wise use of time means knowing when to stop viewing because a site is no longer helpful. As Yell (1998) states, "It is important to realize that the Internet is not a panacea, nor is it a substitute for the law library. It is, however, an extremely valuable tool for the legal researcher."

Table 2.
Selected Law Websites on the Internet

ACLU Students	www.aclu.org/students/
California Administrative Code	ccr.oal.gov
California Codes	www.leginfo.ca.gov/calaw.html
California Courts	www.courtinfo.ca.gov
California Department of Education	goldmine.cde.ca.gov
California Education Law Report	www.mcn.org/a/celr
Cecil Greek's Law Sites	www.fsu.edu/~crimdo/other.html
Chief State School Officers Council	www.ccsso.org
50 States Statutes and Legislation	www.prairienet.org/~scruffy/f.htm
FindLaw California	california.findlaw.com
FindLaw's Law Crawler	lawcrawler.findlaw.com/
John Burton's Cyberspace Bookmarks	www.fontana.k12.ca.us/burton/
John Burton's Links on Expulsion	www.fontana.k12.ca.us/burton/ expulsion.html
Ken Lane's Educational Law Links	http://dcr.csusb.edu/soe/klane (Click on "Links")
LawLinks: Internet Legal Resource Center	www.lawlinks.com
Legal Search Engines and Tools	www.lawguru.com/
Library of Congress	lcweb.loc.gov/
LOIS Law Library	www.pita.com/
National Archives & Records Administration	www.access.gpo.gov/nara/cfr/
The National Law Journal	www.ljextra.com/nlj/
Orange County Public Law Library	www.oc.ca.gov/lawlib/
Special Education: Section 504	www.edlaw.net/frames.html
Supreme Court Decisions:	
1990-present	supct.law.cornell.edu/supct/
1937-1975	www.fedworld.gov/supcourt/index.htm
1893-present	http://www.findlaw.com/casecode/ supreme.html
1000 most cited since 1793	http://www.usscplus.com/topk/index.htm
U.S. Court of Appeals, 9th Circuit: 1995-date	www.ca9.uscourts.gov/
U.S. Department of Education	www.ed.gov
U.S. Code	www4.law.cornell.edu/uscode/
U. S. House of Representatives Internet Law Library	uscode.house.gov/home.htm
U. S. Tax Code	www.fourmilab.ch/ustax/

Recording the Information

After locating a relevant case, the researcher must record its essential elements so that the case is clearly understandable. An excellent template for recording information has been developed by Alexander and Alexander (1998) and is presented in the instructor's guide that accompanies their book. This template enables a researcher to record the important parts of a case and then write it in a brief form as follows:

Parts of a Case

Citation: The names of the plaintiffs and defendants and the location of the case itself are set forth in a standard, much abbreviated, form. The following case was decided by the Supreme Court of Washington on April 6, 1967. It may be found in volume 426 of the *Pacific Reporter*, *Second Series*, beginning on page 471. If a case has been appealed, each court decision will be listed.

Chappel v. Franklin Pierce Sch. Dist. 426 P.2d 471 (Wash. 1967)

Résumé of the Case: A brief statement summarizes the cause of action, relief sought, lower court findings, holding of the present court, and final action.

Headnotes: The publisher places from one to several headnotes at the beginning of each case. Each headnote states a point of law from the case as interpreted by the publisher. Key numbers beside each headnote indicate the subject or issue dealt with; for example, Civil Rights Key Note 3; Constitutional Law, 21 1; Constitutional Law 224 (sex discrimination cases); Schools 172.

Counsel: Attorneys of record for each party are then listed.

Facts: Next comes the court's summary of the facts of the case. In a court of appeal, the facts are not usually disputed. Rather, the issue on appeal is whether the lower court made an error *in law*—whether the appellant had a fair trial.

Name of Judge: If there is more than one opinion, the name of the judge who wrote the majority opinion appears at the beginning of the facts.

Numbers in Text: Portions of the text of the decision show numbers that match the headnotes. In addition, footnotes provide explanatory material and references to other cases.

Body of the Decision: The reasoning and decision of the court may extend from one or two pages to as many as 130. This is the majority opinion. A researcher's challenge is to identify the basis for the decision on each issue.

Concurring Opinions: A judge who agrees with the majority opinion may nevertheless have slightly different reasons for his or her position. His or her individual points are set forth in a concurring opinion.

Dissenting Opinions: If one or more judges disagree with the majority opinion, a dissenting opinion may be filed to set forth that judge's conclusion and explain his or her reasoning. Sometimes the dissents exceed the majority opinions in length, as occurred in the *Rodriguez* case. Of course, only the majority opinion carries the weight of law.

Finding of the Court: The action of a court of appeal may be to affirm the lower court's action, reverse, affirm in part, reverse in part, or reverse and remand for a new trial on the merits of the case.

Sample Brief

Following is a sample legal brief summarizing a school law case that was decided by the Supreme Court of California in 1984.

Citation: *Hartzell v. Connell*
Supreme Court of California, In Bank, 1984
35 Cal.3d 899, 201 Cal.Rptr. 601, 679 P.2d 35

Issue: Imposition of fees for educational extracurricular activities violates the free school guarantee in the California constitution.

Facts: The Santa Barbara High School District offered a wide range of extracurricular activities, including 38 athletic teams. Prior to the 1980-81 school year, students could participate in these activities free of charge. In 1981 the school board cut its budget by $1.1 million, part of which was a reduction in financial support for extracurricular activities. To make the budget work, the ninth-grade athletic program was cut, and students were charged fees ($25) for participation in each dramatic production, musical performance, or athletic competition. The students did not receive credit toward graduation for participation in any of these extracurricular activities. Also, upon showing financial need, a student could have the fees waived. Barbara Hartzell, a taxpayer with two children in the public schools, together with the Coalition Opposing Student Fees, a group of community organizations, filed a lawsuit against the district, various school officials, and members of the school board.

Finding of the Court: The state constitutional provision for free public education prohibits charging fees for either regular or extracurricular programs.

Reasoning: The courts have emphasized the vital importance of student participation in extracurricular activities as part of their educational experience. Group activities encourage participation in community affairs, promote development of leadership qualities, and instill a spirit of collective endeavor. Students should not have the stigma of being needy recorded on public records.

Summary

Legal research involves finding statutes, regulations, law cases, law reviews, and legal interpretations. This chapter has defined the difference between primary and secondary sources of information. The chapter also included information on using a law library and the Internet to research the law.

Knowing how to conduct legal research and where to go for information—whether that be the law library or Internet sources—gives teachers and administrators an immense advantage. They can quickly find current information to address immediate issues in the educational setting. This skill is of tremendous value in providing leadership to faculty, students, and community. A well-known admonition states, "Knowledge is Power!" One should never underestimate the value of knowledge!

Key Terms

1. bookmark
2. California Reporter
3. citations
4. Federal Reporter
5. LEXIS/NEXIS
6. primary sources
7. secondary sources
8. Shepard's Citations
9. United States Code (U.S.C.)
10. West's digest system

Discussion / Essay Questions

1. What are the advantages of utilizing secondary sources when researching legal documents? The disadvantages?

2. Which of the Internet databases of U.S. Supreme Court decisions is easiest to search?

3. What are bookmarks and how are they useful?

4. Go to the Internet site at www.courtinfo.ca.gov. Select a topic of interest to you and write a brief summary of what you find.

5. Conduct a search of California Supreme Court cases involving student attendance. Write a brief of one case.

References

Alexander, K., & Alexander, D. (1998). *American public school law* (4th ed.). St. Paul, MN: West.

Ballard Spahr Andrews & Ingersoll, LLP. (1999). *The virtual chase: A research site for legal professionals*. Website on the World Wide Web at http://www.virtualchase.com/

Chapman, B. (2000). *Brief introduction to using the World Wide Web to conduct legal research*. Available on the World Wide Web at http://www.personal.utulsa.edu/~benjamin-chapman/cle/weblaw.html

Lane, K. E. (1999). Personal homepage on the World Wide Web at dcr.csusb.edu/soe/klane/

West Group. (2000). *Westlaw white paper: Information on your terms*. Retrieved from the World Wide Web at http://www.westlaw.com/ProductsInfo/whitepap.wl

Yell, M. L. (1998). *The law and special education*. Upper Saddle River, NJ: Prentice Hall.

Chapter 3

School Governance and the Law

Introduction

The opening chapter of this book discussed the sources of the laws that govern school districts—the statutes, the regulations, the decisions, and the precedents that give direction to school and district governance. This direction is provided by federal and state legislative bodies, federal and state courts, and federal and state administrative agencies.

This chapter is about governance, or managing the school district. *Black's,* (1999) defines "government" as "an organization through which a body of people exercise political authority; the machinery by which sovereign power is expressed." If one could compare the governance of a local school district with the federal or state government, the school board fills the role of the legislative branch. It is the board's job to establish policy, or make the law. The superintendent of schools has the role of a president or governor in that it is his or her job to abide by the policies of the board and to manage the district.

A student of government quickly learns that the roles of Congress, the President, and the federal courts are not clearly defined. The three branches of government often find themselves in conflict, charging one another with infringement of responsibility. This same situation often occurs with the governor, legislature and courts at the state level.

Similarly, the lines for governance of schools are not always clear. Misunderstanding, confusion, and conflict may exist between the local school district board and its superintendent. Their roles may blend or overlap. Often, a superintendent assumes the role of establishing policies or regulations that govern the district. Occasionally, a school board assumes, or largely assumes, the management role of the superintendent. By keeping this reality in mind, the reader will appreciate that the governmental agencies with prime responsibility for implementing the law occasionally appear to create law as well. This chapter focuses on the bodies that most influence the governance of a school district: the California State Board of Education and State Superintendent of Public Instruction, the county boards of education and county superintendents of schools, and the local boards of education and school district superintendents.

California State Board of Education

The 1879 California constitution established a state Board of Education, which consists of ten members appointed by the Governor for a term of four years. A student member, appointed for a term of one year, also sits on the board. State Board of Education appointments must be made with the advice and consent of two-thirds of the state senate. The executive officer of the state Board of Education is required to keep a record of its proceedings and take charge of its correspondence. Education Code sections 33000-33080 specify the composition and requirements of the state board. Section 33032 provides direction to the state board:

> The board shall study the educational conditions and needs of the state. It shall make plans for the improvement of the administration and efficiency of the public schools of the state.

An important function of the state board is to grant waivers of Education Code sections to California school districts. A waiver is defined as "an exemption from a requirement of the Education Code." For example, California requires 175 days of student school attendance each year (E.D. 41420). However, a district that experiences an earthquake, a flood, or some other natural disaster may request the state Board of Education to waive the 175-day requirement. The state board has considered an array of waiver requests, from changing the days required to celebrate a national holiday to housing students in non-Field Act (non-earthquake-compliant) buildings.

Occasionally, the state board and State Superintendent of Public Instruction have clashed over the philosophy and direction of education. Since the State Superintendent of Public Instruction is elected, he or she has a certain degree of independence from the state board. In recent times, the most publicized clash between the state board and the State Superintendent of Public Instruction occurred when Bill Honig served as state Superintendent, although Superintendent Delaine Eastin has also had serious differences of opinion with the board.

State Superintendent of Public Instruction

The 1849 California constitution provided for a popularly elected Superintendent of Public Instruction. The original term of office of three years was changed to four years in 1862. In 1990, the office was limited to two consecutive terms as part of Proposition 140, a general term-limit measure.

Education Code sections 33100 through 33193 establish the powers and duties of the position. As noted above, the State Superintendent serves as secretary to the state Board of Education. In addition, he or she is *ex officio* Director of Education. In this role, the Superintendent is responsible for carrying out the policies of the state board. He or she is to provide leadership to county and district school superintendents and has financial responsibility for estimating the amount of state school funds to be apportioned to each county. The Superintendent is also the chief state spokesperson in relation to the U.S. Department of Education.

In 1988 California citizens added duties to the job description of the state Superintendent. Proposition 98—which was supported by a coalition of teachers, administrators, school board members, and members of the Parent Teacher Association—established the School Accountability Report Card. Each California district was required to develop this report card each year for review by parents and citizens of the district. The Superintendent was responsible for overseeing implementation of this requirement.

Proposition 98 also gave the Superintendent additional fiscal oversight of school districts. In consequence of more than 30 California school districts becoming insolvent, the state Superintendent was given responsibility for working with county superintendents to monitor and review local school district budgets. Should a school district become insolvent, the state Superintendent appoints an administrator to manage the local district. This administrator reports directly to the State Superintendent. While the district is under state control, the appointed administrator assumes the authority normally assigned to the local district board of education

The prime example of an insolvent district is Compton Unified School District, which has been under state control for the last several years. Coachella Unified School District, in Riverside County, is another example of a district that was placed under state control due to financial insolvency. Richmond Unified School District was placed under state control in 1991, as shown in Table 1, chapter 1.

County Boards of Education

The county board of education is another entity involved in the governance of school districts. This body was established by the state legislature in 1879. The organizational procedures and duties of the county board are included in Education Code sections 1000 through 1097. A county board may have either five or seven members, as determined by the County Committee on School District Organization. Board members are elected by trustee area. The duties of the board are contained in Education Code section 1040:

1. adopt rules and regulations, consistent with the laws of this state, for their own government
2. keep a record of their proceedings
3. approve the annual budget of the county superintendent of schools before its submission to the county board of supervisors
4. approve the annual county school service fund budget of the county superintendent of schools before its submission to the State Superintendent of Public Instruction
5. review at a regularly scheduled public meeting the annual audit provided for by the county superintendent of schools, including an audit of each district in the county.

The county office plays a major role in providing assistance to local districts. Its support is particularly needed in smaller districts. Some of its services include business and personnel management; special education, library, audiovisual, and health services; and assistance in developing and implementing instructional programs.

A major function of the county office is to provide credential services for teachers in local school districts. Prior to issuing a warrant for services, each county office is required to certify that teachers have met credential requirements in that county. In recent years an expanding role of the county has been to provide financial assistance and advice to school districts and to serve as a "watch dog" over their fiscal solvency.

County Superintendent of Schools

County superintendents play a significant role in governing and regulating local school districts. This office has become particularly important in fiscal monitoring and control. The position of county superintendent was established by the 1849 California constitution. The superintendent may either be elected by the people or appointed by the county board of education.

The state legislature establishes the qualifications for the position; these vary with the size of the county. The qualifications for county superintendent, along with the duties and responsibilities of the office, are contained in Education Code Sections 1200 through 1281.

Parallel to the duties of the State Superintendent of Public Instruction are the responsibilities of the county superintendent of schools as *ex officio* secretary and executive officer of the county board of education. General duties of the county superintendent are contained in section 1240 of the Education Code:

1. supervise the schools of his or her county
2. visit each school at reasonable intervals to observe its operation and to learn of its problems and, if desired, present an annual report to the county board and the county board of supervisors
3. distribute all laws, reports, circulars, instructions, and forms that he or she may receive for the use of the school officers
4. preserve all reports of the Superintendent of Public Instruction
5. keep a record of his or her official acts, and of all the proceedings of the County Board of Education
6. enforce the course of study
7. enforce the use of state-adopted elementary textbooks and of high school textbooks regularly adopted by the proper authority
8. preserve carefully all reports of school officers and teachers
9. deliver to his or her successor all documents belonging to the office
10. submit two financial reports per year to the County Board of Education certifying that his or her office can meet its financial obligations for the current and subsequent fiscal year
11. if requested, act as agent to purchase supplies for city and high school districts in the county

12. report to the Commission on Teaching Credentialing the identity of any certificated person who knowingly and willingly reports false fiscal expenditure data

The county superintendent was assigned significantly greater responsibility for school district budgets in 1991 with the passage of Assembly Bill 1200. This legislation gave the county superintendent authority to audit the expenditures and financial affairs of school districts in the county, as noted above.

Local Boards of Education

In all states except Hawaii, state legislatures have delegated the day-to-day supervision and operation of schools to local boards of education. These boards have the authority granted to them by the state constitution and legislative action. Their responsibilities usually include developing and enforcing policies, employing personnel, and managing the financial affairs of the district. Actions of a local board must fall within the legal boundaries established by federal and state constitutions, statutes, and court decisions.

California's Education Code Section 35010 establishes control of school districts by a local governing board: "Every school district shall be under the control of a board of school trustees or a board of education." The general public typically uses the phrase "school boards" (Wenkart, 1995).

A school district's governing board may exercise its powers and must take all actions authorized or required only at properly noticed meetings open to the public (Education Code sections 35140 and 35145). Minutes shall be taken at each meeting of the board, and all actions taken by the governing board must be recorded in the minutes and made available to the public (Education Code section 35145). Extensive statutory rules and regulations, enumerated in sections in the 35000 series of the Education Code, must be followed. The reader interested in this voluminous set of regulations is advised to review the relevant sections.

Education Code section 35107 establishes eligibility for election or appointment as a member of a local school board. The requirements are as follows:

- eighteen years of age or older
- a citizen of California
- a resident of the district
- a registered voter

- not disqualified by the constitution or laws of the state from holding civil office.

School board elections are scheduled every two years, and board members are elected for a four-year term. Generally, the governing board of a school district has five members elected at large by the voters of the district. However, in certain instances a board may consist of three members or seven. For details regarding the number of members of the local board, see Education Code section 35012.

Generally, school board elections are held the first Tuesday after the first Monday in November in odd-numbered years (Education Code section 5000). Board members may be compensated for service. The key word in section 35120 of the Education Code is "may." The board "may" approve a resolution establishing board compensation. Once compensation has been established, its amount is set by the Education Code, based on the size of the district. Compensation may range from $2,000 per month in Los Angeles Unified School District (average daily attendance of 400,000 or greater) to $60 per month in a district with less than 150 average daily attendance.

School District Superintendent

The Governing Board of any school district that employs at least eight teachers may also employ a district superintendent, delegating specified duties to him or her (Education Code section 35026). One of a board's most important responsibilities is to appoint a competent superintendent of schools. The superintendent is the executive officer of the school system, whereas the board is the legislative, policymaking body. Because the board consists of laypersons who are not experts in school management, it is the responsibility of the board to see that management of the district is properly performed by professional personnel.

The primary duties of a district superintendent are spelled out in Education Code section 35035:

1. serve as chief executive officer of the governing board of the district
2. prepare and submit the district's budget to the governing board
3. make appropriate assignment of all district certificated employees
4. implement district policy regarding transfer of teachers from one site to another

5. ensure that employees in certificated positions hold the required credentials
6. enter into contracts for and on behalf of the district, subject to ratification of the governing board
7. submit required financial and budget reports.

A major function of the superintendent is to gather and present information so that school board members can make intelligent policy decisions. In addition, the superintendent is responsible for the day-to-day operation of the schools within the district and serves as the major public spokesperson for the schools. The superintendent advises the board and keeps members informed of the status of new legislation, student achievement, and fiscal and personnel matters. The larger the school district, the greater the reliance of a board on its superintendent.

The superintendent's powers are broad, and the duties many and diverse. The power and influence of the school superintendent vary greatly from district to district, depending upon several elements. These include the management style and personality of the individual who holds the position, the make-up of the local school board, the history and traditions of the district, the length of time the superintendent has held the position, the number of years remaining on his or her contract, and a variety of other factors. In some districts the relationship between the superintendent and board is tenuous. When there is continued disagreement or a major conflict over policy between the board and the superintendent, the superintendent is usually replaced.

As the above description suggests, the scope and style of superintendent leadership differ from district to district. Some individuals who hold the position are referred to as "strong superintendents." This phrase usually means that the superintendent makes managerial decisions in fiscal, personnel, and curriculum areas, fully expecting board support and approval. This type of superintendent is usually proactive, a take-charge individual who may not always wait for board approval prior to action. The strong superintendent may even present some decisions to the board for ratification or approval after the fact.

Other superintendents are referred to as "weak." This adjective usually means that the superintendent sees his or her role as simply to implement the directions of the board. With this leadership style, most significant decisions are made with prior board approval. Obviously, the contrast of strong with weak superintendents is just one means of demonstrating the great variance that exists in this leadership role. Most school superintendents probably fall near the middle of the continuum, being perceived as strong on some issues and less strong on others.

Principals

Principals are often compared to middle managers in private industry. The man or woman who holds this position is responsible for the day-to-day management of the school. The scope of the leadership role of the principal is broad. In addition to daily management of the myriad activities of students, teachers, and staff, a principal is expected to provide leadership in curriculum, personnel, and school finance. On any given day, the activities of a principal may range from supervising bus duty in the morning to attending a town meeting in the evening in hopes of influencing the fate of a bond election.

Basic leadership research confirms that if the policies established by the state legislature, State Superintendent of Public Instruction, and the local board and superintendent are to be successfully implemented, it is the leadership ability of the principal that will make it happen.

Summary

This chapter has described the governance of education from the state level to school district management. Discussion of the several governmental entities clarifies their roles and responsibilities in school governance. For example, the state legislature, state Board of Education, county boards of education, and local school district governing boards are all legislative bodies that set policy.

However, responsibility for managing schools and school districts resides with the executive branch of government, which is to say the State Superintendent of Public Instruction, the several county superintendents, and superintendents and principals in local districts. All these entities have responsibility for implementing the statutes and court decisions affecting schools. However, just as the lines of authority and responsibility are not always clear among the Congress, federal courts, and the President, the lines for governance of schools are sometimes unclear as well.

Key Terms

1. Assembly Bill 1200
2. board minutes
3. county board of education
4. county superintendent of schools
5. governing board
6. school principal
7. school superintendent
8. state Board of Education
9. State Superintendent of Public Instruction
10. waivers

Discussion / Essay Questions

1. A county superintendent of schools has a major role in providing services to local school districts. What do you consider to be the most important service provided by the county superintendent? Why?

2. What are the qualifications for election or appointment to a school board? Do you think any qualifications should be changed or added? If so, please discuss your suggested changes.

3. School board members may be compensated for services as a board member. Do you agree or disagree with this concept? State your rationale for this answer.

4. The State Superintendent of Public Instruction in California is an elected position. Do you believe that an elected state Superintendent provides the best service for students, or would services improve if the position were appointed by the state Board of Education? Give the rationale for your answer.

5. There is a high rate of turnover in the office of school district superintendent. Discuss at least three reasons for this phenomenon.

References

Black's Law Dictionary (7th ed.). (1999). Bryan A. Garner, Editor-in-Chief. St. Paul, MN: West Group.

Wenkart, R. (1995). *The California educators' guide to school law* (2nd ed.). Costa Mesa, CA: Orange County Department of Education.

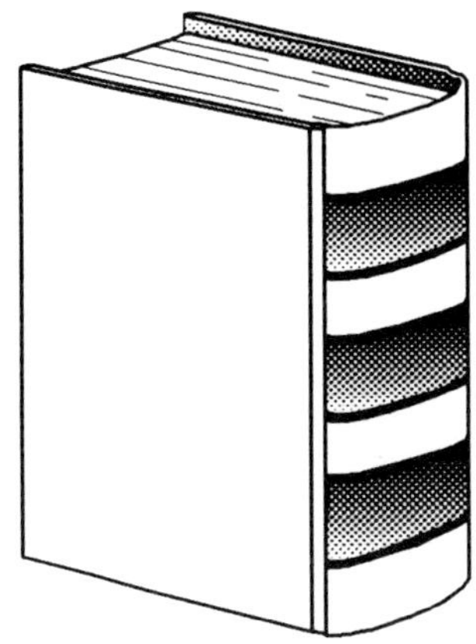

Chapter 4

Student Citizenship and Discipline

Introduction

All students have the right to a free public education. At first this statement seems straightforward and unambiguous. As one imagines an array of students representing various learning needs and personal goals, however, that simple principle becomes challenging, complex, and open to a variety of interpretations. Federal and state legislative bodies have produced voluminous laws in an attempt to clarify the meaning of "free public education." At one time in the nation's history, females and various ethnic groups were excluded from such education. Currently, the nature of free appropriate public education for bilingual students and immigrants is strongly debated. The amount of education has also been subject to interpretation: Does the concept extend to preschool and kindergarten? Should public education end only after eighth grade, twelfth grade, two years of college, a bachelor's or master's degree, or even the doctorate?

Curriculum content has also been the subject of much debate. Should free public education be limited to basic skills of reading, writing, and arithmetic? What about the study of religion, sex education, the arts, etc.? This debate has not been resolved. These issues are often of major concern to parents, citizens, school boards, educators, legislators, and the courts. However important they may be, in recent years these concerns have been overshadowed by a frightening and urgent worry: how to ensure a student's right to attend a school that is safe and free of violence.

A 1993 National School Boards Association study concluded that school violence had reached epidemic proportions. More than three quarters, 82%, of the 1,979 school districts polled in that study reported an increase in violence during the preceding five years (Smith, 1994). A 1993 study by the U.S. Justice Department reached a similar conclusion. Reacting to the study, Attorney General Janet Reno said, "Unless we act now to stop young people from choosing a life of violent crime, the beginning of the 21st century could bring levels of violent crime to our cities that far exceed what we have experienced." The attorney general said she was shocked by the rise in the murder rate among 14- to 17-year-olds: 165% in the previous decade ("U.S. Juvenile Crime," 1995).

A 1993 Harris poll of students in grades six through twelve found widespread fear of violence at school. This fear is not unfounded. In a study by Batsche and Knoff (1994), one in seven students reported that they had been bullied, and one in twelve middle or high school students had stayed home from school in fear of being attacked at school. More than 400,000 violent crimes are reported in and around our nation's schools each year, with still more crimes going unreported (Chancellor's Working Group, 1994).

Beatings and even murder of students on school campuses has happened all too often. For example, the Superintendent of Washington DC public schools reported 59 physical assaults against teachers and students in that district in 1993-1994. Thirty-two guns were confiscated from students, and there were seven shootings in and around schools (Smith, 1994).

An examination of violence as an emerging problem in education was presented in *Violent Schools—Safe Schools* (National Institute of Education, 1978). This publication brought about a better understanding of the nature and extent of violence in American education. Approximately 12% (125,000) of the secondary teachers surveyed had been threatened with physical harm in a school month, and many of the teachers hesitated to confront disruptive students for fear of physical harm.

Verbal abuse of teachers was common. One-half of all the surveyed teachers mentioned that they had been abused verbally several times in a typical month. The issue of school violence became the focus of the National Education Goals Panel (1993) as members proposed that by the year 2000 "Every school in America will be free of drugs and violence and will offer a disciplined environment conducive to learning."

As the above information indicates, in many schools and classrooms it has become difficult for teachers to teach and for students to learn because of poor student citizenship. In recent surveys, 41% of teachers reported losing "a fair amount of teaching time because of discipline problems" (Pasternak, 1995). Many students show little respect for teacher authority and make proper classroom management difficult for the teacher.

America's Response to School Citizenship Problems

Americans are sharply divided on how students, both in and out of school, should be disciplined and controlled. Parents, citizens, legislative bodies, and the courts have responded to the concern over student citizenship in a variety of ways. On the one hand, the U.S. Supreme Court appears to give schools great latitude in disciplining students, while at the same time asserting, as in *Tinker v. Des Moines Independent Community School District* (1969), that children in school are persons who do not shed their Constitutional rights at the schoolhouse door. In this landmark case, the Supreme Court ruled in a seven-to-two decision that the district could not ban black armbands worn by students in protest against the Vietnam War.

Tinker specifically held that schools cannot suppress speech "because of an undifferentiated fear or apprehension of disturbance." To justify suppression of a student's right to free speech, the Court ruled that a school must prove that the student's First Amendment exercise would "materially and substantially" disrupt the school program.

The Supreme Court further clarified the material and substantial disruption standard in *Bethel School District No. 403 v. Fraser* (1986). In that case, a high school student gave a speech before the student body that was full of graphic and sexually explicit language. The student had been warned regarding the inappropriateness of the speech. Fraser, the high school student, received a three-day suspension for violating a school rule prohibiting the use of obscene language. The Court found a marked distinction between the student's speech in Fraser and the students' armbands in Tinker. Fraser's speech, the Court determined, did not merit First Amendment protection. Therefore, school administrators had the authority to suppress his free speech rights. The Court concluded, "It is a highly appropriate function of a public school education to prohibit the use of vulgar and offensive terms in public discourse."

In 1994 a California court decided that schools can discipline students for inappropriate behavior that could lead to further disruption (*Lovell v. Poway Unified School District*, 1994). Lovell, a high school student, allegedly threatened to shoot a counselor. The court decided that in order to support an expulsion or suspension, the statement must indicate that the student possesses an intent to harm or assault. In the Lovell case, the court could find no such intent. Nonetheless, the court stated that a school board could impose boundaries on a student's free speech rights by prohibiting threats of physical injury.

A recent Supreme Court ruling, *Vernonia School District v. Acton* (1995), affirms the constitutionality of giving schools the right to search students. Judge ɔte that "the expectation of privacy of minors is not as great as that of . He cited mandatory physical examinations and vaccinations by public ɹools as "legitimate intrusions." He further added, "A 'reasonable' search does not have to be the least intrusive search in order to pass muster under the Fourth Amendment."

The question facing policy leaders in this country is how to achieve safe schools and at what cost to the nation's taxpayers. Educators have proposed a multitude of solutions to the problem. A highly favored proposal made by teachers is reduction of class size so they can devote greater attention to correcting student misbehavior. Other stakeholders have advocated funding for both preschool and parent education and an increased number of counselors and psychologists at school sites. A strong plea has been made for resources to support development of new programs to cope with misconduct by younger students at elementary schools.

Americans have not made a strong commitment to financing preventive programs. State legislatures and school boards are increasing reliance on suspension and expulsion as the weapons of choice in the battle to keep schools safe. States and school districts, prompted by a federal mandate to keep guns out of schools and an increasing public outcry against violence on campuses, are passing strict student citizenship policies.

Texas and New York have approved bills to banish students who carry guns and knives to school. Another dozen states were expected to join the no-weapons push in 1995 (Portner, 1995). In spring of 1999 an article in *USA Today* reported that 90% of schools had zero-tolerance policies for weapons and 87%, for alcohol and drugs (Cauchon, 1999). One can surmise that the nation's founding fathers would be shocked to learn about drive-by shootings at school campuses or six-year-olds being expelled from school for possessing a pocketknife.

In spite of statistics showing an alarming increase in student misbehavior and serious disciplinary problems on many school campuses, the authors have observed that public schools have rarely regarded a misbehavior as serious enough to warrant expulsion from the district. This is especially the case in America's elementary schools.

However, a relatively small percentage of disruptive students can wreak havoc in a classroom or on a school campus. Therefore, schools and districts have begun to institute innovative instructional and management programs to cope with disruptive students. Such programs do not fall within the purview of a textbook on education law, but are well worth investigation by school administrators, not only when faced by school disruption, but to prevent its occurrence.

The remainder of this chapter focuses on student behavior and discipline measures to ensure a safe and orderly campus. Such measures are employed by teachers, administrators, and school boards to ensure well-managed classrooms in which students can study and learn without peer misconduct distracting from the process.

Student Discipline

"Student discipline starts at home." Although there is little disagreement with this statement among most Americans, parents and educators are engaged in a great debate about expectations for student citizenship.

Student fighting is a good example. Every principal is confronted at one time or another by a parent who, when his or her child has been in a fight, proclaims that the student has always been told to "punch out" a student who calls him a name or pushes him while in the lunch line. Both teachers and administrators have heard the parent of a perennially tardy student exclaim, "I just can't get her to school on time!"

More students than ever before enter school suffering from emotional and physical neglect. In many cases, little citizenship education has been provided in the home. Respect for privacy or property and the general rules of civility seem virtually unknown to many children and their parents. Children who enter school from such environments are a challenge to the teacher and the school system. Their disregard for school rules makes it difficult for a teacher to teach and for other students to learn.

Those who attribute increasing student misbehavior to lack of supervision have many statistics to cite. For example, as noted in an article in the *Los Angeles Times*, the proportion of single-parent families nearly doubled between 1970 and 1995, from 13% to 24%. This represented four out of every ten children. In just one generation the number of children born out of wedlock increased five times. Finally, "a leading social scientist says American parents spend about 40% less time with their children than did parents of a generation ago" (Marshall, 1995).

Rules and Procedures

Clear, consistently enforced expectations and rules are necessary for effective classroom management and instruction. Teachers have always established classroom rules, but as society has become more complex, schools and local school boards have written policies to regulate student behavior. State legislatures, too, have become more prescriptive in setting expectations for student conduct. For example, the fornia Education Code, section 233.5, provides general guidance for teachers ,arding the teaching of morals, manners, and citizenship.

> Each teacher shall endeavor to impress upon the minds of the pupils the principles of morality, truth, justice, patriotism, and a true comprehension of the rights, duties, and dignity of American citizenship, and the meaning of equality and human dignity, including the promotion of harmonious relations, kindness toward domestic pets and the humane treatment of living creatures, to teach them to avoid idleness, profanity, and falsehood, and to instruct them in manners and morals and the principles of a free government.

This code section was amended in 1994 when the legislature added the following:

> Each teacher is also encouraged to create and foster an environment that encourages pupils to realize their full potential and that is free from discriminatory attitudes, practices, events, or activities, in order to prevent acts of hate violence.

To assist teachers in achieving this lofty objective, section 48908 requires all pupils to submit to the authority of teachers.

The California legislature requires each school, at least once every four years, to adopt rules and procedures for student discipline (E.C. 35291.5). This code section requires input from a representative chosen by each of the following: parents, teachers, administrators, and school security personnel. At junior and senior high schools, student input is also required. The rules must be consistent with state law and district policy. The final set of rules is to be approved by the principal or designee and a representative selected by classroom teachers. After the rules are adopted, the principal is required to provide parents with a copy of them at the beginning of each school year.

The California Administrative Code (Title V) also provides direction for student conduct:

> Every pupil shall attend school punctually and regularly; conform to the regulations of the school; obey promptly all the directions of his teacher and others in authority; observe good order and propriety of deportment; be diligent in study, respectful to his teacher and others in

> authority, kind and courteous to schoolmates; and refrain entirely from the use of profane and vulgar language.

Title V regulations also address such issues as student cleanliness, dress, and care of property:

> A pupil who goes to school without proper attention to personal cleanliness or neatness of dress may be sent home to be properly prepared for school, or shall be required to prepare himself for the schoolroom before entering.

> A pupil who defaces, damages, or destroys any school property or willfully or negligently injures another pupil or school employee is liable to suspension or expulsion, according to the nature of the offense.

In Loco Parentis

Teachers and school districts are granted wide discretion in disciplining students by the courts. The legal doctrine that defines the relationship of a teacher to a pupil is *in loco parentis* (Latin for "in place of parent").

The California legislature elaborated the principle of *in loco parentis* in section 44807 of the Education Code:

> Every teacher in the public schools shall hold pupils to a strict account for their conduct on the way to and from school, on the playgrounds, or during recess. A teacher, vice principal, principal, or any other certificated employee of a school district, shall not be subject to criminal prosecution or criminal penalties for the exercise, during the performance of his duties, of the same degree of physical control over a pupil that a parent would be legally privileged to exercise but which in no event shall exceed the amount of physical control reasonably necessary to maintain order, protect property, or protect the health and safety of pupils, or to maintain proper and appropriate conditions conducive to learning.

Parent Support

"If you get in trouble at school, you will be in bigger trouble at home." Most adults over age 40 are familiar with this admonition from parents. For many decades, this warning assisted teachers and principals in maintaining proper citizenship in classrooms and schools. However, at some point in the nation's history, the partnership between parents and teachers began to diminish.

Scholars who study children and their performance in schools attribute the decrease in parental support for teachers and schools to a variety of factors. Sociologists may charge this lack of cooperation between schools and parents to an increased number of mothers who are members of the labor force, thus no longer available to supervise their children. Fathers who still live in the two-parent home also seem to have less time for the child. A recent study found that more than half the fathers questioned were spending less than five minutes with their children on a typical workday (Marshall, 1995).

Psychologists may cite the increase in drug use among parents and students as a cause of increased student misbehavior. They may also identify an increase in the number of students who are living in one-parent homes as a cause of reduced supervision of students. Political scientists attribute an increase in student misbehavior to loss of respect for schools along with loss of respect for all governmental agencies.

While scholars will long debate the reasons for the decrease in student and parent respect for teachers, seasoned teachers testify that it has occurred. They also confirm that it is more difficult to gain the cooperation of parents when disciplining a misbehaving child than it once was. They verify that it is more difficult to motivate many parents to attend conferences and to respond to telephone calls or written notices.

Many teachers feel that attempting to contact parents about student misbehavior is non-productive. One reason is that, with the increase in one-parent families, teachers find they cannot readily reach the parent by phone. Arranging parent conferences to discuss student academic achievement or student behavior is also difficult. Secondly, a note sent home with the student, or even through the mail, often does not reach the parent's hand. Finally, if contact is achieved, many parents are unable to provide much assistance in coping with an unruly student. Due to their personal or professional situation, many parents are unable to supervise the student consistently or to offer incentives for improved citizenship.

Corrective Behavior and/or Punishment

If a student breaks the rules, misbehaves, or disrupts the educational program, what action can a teacher, principal, or the school board utilize for correction or punishment? Even with the legal doctrine of *in loco parentis*, the school's authority is limited. In fact, in most states, the classroom teacher is limited to verbal admonitions and reprimands, detention, contacting parents of the child, corporal punishment, and referral to the principal. Moreover, a California teacher is prohibited from corporal punishment as a means of correcting student misconduct (E.C. 48900). The California teacher also has limited ability to suspend a student when misconduct occurs (E.C. 48910).

There is general recognition that the principal is a key figure in maintaining an orderly and safe school. Therefore, the principal has been given greater authority than a teacher to suspend or recommend expulsion of a student as a disciplinary measure.

A superintendent of schools has additional authority, beyond that of a principal, for dealing with disruptive students. He or she may transfer such students, age sixteen or older, to a continuation school. The superintendent also has the power to recommend expulsion of a student (E.C. 48432.5). Finally, the board of education has the authority to expel a student from the jurisdiction of the school district (E.C. 48900). Students and parents must be granted due process in each of these procedures.

Detention

Detention is defined as keeping a child in the classroom or another designated place before school, at recess, during lunch, or after school. The courts have routinely upheld the right of teachers and principals to impose detention on unruly and non-attending students. The teacher is usually responsible for supervising the student during the detention period. However, it has become a common practice in many middle and secondary schools to have a separate room, with a separate staff member, for this purpose.

The teacher's right to assign detention varies from state to state. In California, teachers are prohibited from utilizing detention during recess or the lunch hour. An exception to this limitation is possible if a governing board has adopted rules and regulations authorizing the teacher to restrict for disciplinary purposes the time a student is allowed for recess (E.C. 44807.5). Some schools require students who have misbehaved to stay in the principal's office or another designated area during a portion of the recess period.

In many school districts, teachers are required to give the parent at least one day's notice prior to the student staying for after-school detention. After-school detention is limited to one hour, and a student may not be detained if he or she would miss regular bus transportation.

Corporal Punishment

Corporal punishment is defined as infliction of physical pain for misconduct. State statutes deal with corporal punishment in different ways, some states authorizing it and others forbidding it. Still others are silent on the matter, but by implication allow it (Hudgins, 1985). Massachusetts and New Jersey prohibit corporal punishment by statute. The Maryland State Board of Education forbids it, while New York allows local boards of education to decide.

In the landmark Supreme Court decision *Ingraham v. Wright* (1977), the Court held that corporal punishment of students violates neither the Eighth Amendment nor the due process guarantees of the Fourteenth Amendment. The Court said the Eighth Amendment's prohibition of cruel and unusual punishment applies to criminals only and is not applicable to disciplining students in public schools.

While the merit of utilizing corporal punishment to promote proper student citizenship and correct misbehavior will continue to be debated, this method of discipline is not available to California teachers and administrators. In 1986 section 49001 was added to the California Education Code to prohibit physical punishment: "No person employed by or engaged in a public school shall inflict, or cause to be inflicted corporal punishment upon a pupil." Section 49000 presents the rationale of the legislature for prohibiting corporal punishment:

> The Legislature finds and declares that the protection against corporal punishment, which extends to other citizens in other walks of life, should include children while they are under the control of the public schools. Children of school age are at the most vulnerable and impressionable period of their lives and it is wholly reasonable that the safeguards to the integrity and sanctity of their bodies should be, at this tender age, at least equal to that afforded to other citizens.

The legislature clarified that prohibition of corporal punishment did not preclude teachers and school administrators from utilizing reasonable force to quell a disturbance. Reasonable force can be used when a student is threatening physical injury to another student or a teacher. Reasonable force may also be used when there is a threat to school property. A student's voluntary participation in athletics that results in physical pain was also excluded from the definition of corporal punishment (E.C. 49001).

California's Suspension and Expulsion Laws

The California legislature has been more prescriptive than many other states in specifying types of misbehavior or misconduct for which suspension or expulsion of students is allowed. In 1983 the legislature specified twelve acts for which a student may be suspended from school by a teacher, principal or superintendent. These have subsequently been expanded, the most recent additions involving sexual harassment and sexual assault and battery; hate violence; "terroristic" threats; harassing a student complainant or witness in a disciplinary procedure; harassment, threats, or intimidation with the intent of disrupting the school or invading the rights of another pupil; and carrying an imitation firearm that looks like the real thing (E.C. 48900 through 48900.7).

Although either suspension or expulsion may result from the same misconduct, only a school board has authority to expel a student. Expulsion procedures will be discussed in a later section of this chapter. As the reader would expect, the grounds for suspension and expulsion were written by attorneys and are legal in nature. For purposes of this text, the grounds for suspension and expulsion are simplified and rearranged into groups according to the nature of the offense. As an administrator charged with the responsibility for suspending a student or recommending expulsion, one should review the actual Education Code sections. Students may be suspended or expelled if—on school grounds, going to or from school or a school-sponsored activity, or during the lunch hour, whether on campus or off—they have been involved with

- personal violence

  1. attempting, threatening, or causing physical injury or willfully using force against another person, except in self-defense
  2. attempting, threatening, causing, or participating in hate violence
  3. attempting or committing sexual assault or committing sexual battery

• extortion or harassment

4. attempting or committing extortion
5. making terrorist-like threats against school officials or school property
6. harassing, threatening, or intimidating a pupil who is a complainant or witness in a school disciplinary proceeding
7. intentionally engaging in harassment, threats, or intimidation with the actual and reasonably expected effect of materially disrupting classwork, creating substantial disorder, or invading the rights of other pupils
8. engaging in sexual harassment

• dangerous objects

9. possessing, selling, or otherwise furnishing any firearm, knife, explosive, or other dangerous object
10. possessing an imitation, but realistic, firearm

• drugs, alcohol, or tobacco

11. unlawfully possessing, using, selling, or otherwise furnishing, or being under the influence of a controlled substance, an alcoholic beverage, or an intoxicant of any kind
12. unlawfully offering, arranging, or negotiating to sell and then selling, delivering, or furnishing any controlled substance, alcoholic beverage, intoxicant, or material represented as such a substance
13. unlawfully possessing, offering, arranging, or negotiating to sell drug paraphernalia
14. possessing or using tobacco or products containing tobacco or nicotine

• damage to or theft of property

15. attempting or committing robbery
16. stealing or attempting to steal school or private property
17. knowingly receiving stolen school or private property
18. damaging or attempting to damage school or private property

- disruptive or vulgar behavior

19. committing an obscene act or engaging in habitual profanity or vulgarity
20. disrupting school activities or otherwise willfully defying the valid authority of supervisors, teachers, administrators, school officials, or other school personnel engaged in the performance of their duties.

It is interesting to note that despite the careful attention devoted to the language in the suspension and expulsion laws, parents and attorneys continue to seek loopholes. For example, the Superintendent of the Vista Unified School District recently asked the assemblyman of that district to plug a potential loophole by drafting a bill that would add bomb threats to the list of expellable offenses. Superintendent Jack Gyves made this request after the district had received a number of bomb threats, and a parent made an issue of the fact that there was no specific language in the Education Code forbidding such threats. Gyves said, "95% of the time they're pranks, but when you're emptying a high school of 2,600 students, there are all kinds of opportunity for injury, panic, whatever" (de Vise, 1996).

Suspension from School

Suspension from school is defined as removal of a student from ongoing instruction for adjustment purposes (E.C. 48925). Suspension is one of the most widely used measures of disciplining students, especially at the secondary level. The length of time for suspensions ranges from state to state, usually not exceeding ten days. California limits the maximum length of a single suspension to five days (E.C. 48911), although there are some exceptions. For example, a student who is being recommended to the school board for expulsion may be suspended while the expulsion is being considered. A longer suspension is also possible when the presence of the pupil constitutes a danger to persons or property or threatens to disrupt the instructional process or if a child is truly dangerous.

In contrast to detailed procedures for the expulsion of a student, state statutes are less specific regarding the procedures that should be followed when suspending students from school. Prior to 1975 procedural due process accorded to suspended students was poorly defined. Lower courts differed widely in their interpretation of Fourteenth Amendment guarantees in suspension cases. In 1975, however, the U.S. Supreme Court prescribed the minimum Constitutional requirements in cases involving student suspension of ten days or less (*Goss v. Lopez*, 1975).

The Court concluded that a student should be given an oral or written notice of the charge and, if he or she denies the charge, an opportunity to provide an explanation of the evidence. Compliance with these requirements would meet the due process requirement for a brief suspension. For suspensions, the Court specifically rejected the usual trial-type format that would include involvement of attorneys and presentation and cross-examination of adverse witnesses, as is typical in criminal cases.

The courts give school districts considerable latitude in use of suspensions to maintain discipline. For example, *Abella v. Riverside Unified School District* (1976) established the following authority for California school districts:

> A school district has the authority to maintain discipline in the schools and to that end, may suspend or expel a pupil who refuses or neglects to obey any rules prescribed pursuant to the Education Code as long as the authority is exercised in a manner that will satisfy the statutory and constitutional standards for disciplinary proceedings.

Legislative Guidelines and Limitations for Suspensions and Expulsions

Even with the wide latitude granted by the courts to use suspensions to correct student misbehavior, some limitations are placed on a principal or superintendent when suspending or expelling students. Authority with regard to the location of the offense is broad: A student may be suspended or expelled for misbehavior related to school activity or attendance while on school grounds; while going to or coming from school; during the lunch period whether on or off the campus; and during, or while going to or coming from, a school-sponsored activity. However, the act states that application of suspension or expulsion is not limited to these four situations.

On the other hand, the legislature placed a limitation on school boards and administrators by declaring its intent that alternatives to suspension and expulsion should be imposed for students who are truant, tardy, or absent from school activities (E.C. 48900). When E.C. 48900.6 was added in 1993, principals and superintendents were presented with one such alternative—authority to require a student to perform community service on school grounds during non-school hours in lieu of suspension. Community service could include work in the areas of outdoor beautification, campus betterment, and teacher or peer assistance programs.

With a few exceptions, districts may not suspend a student for more than twenty school days in any school year. Exceptions may occur if a student enrolls in or is transferred to another regular school, an opportunity school or class, or a continuation education school or class. In these cases, the maximum number of days a student may be suspended is increased to thirty within a school year (E.C. 48903). A governing board may also suspend a student enrolled in a continuation school or class for the remainder of the semester. Depending upon when the offense occurred, this time limit may exceed twenty days (E.C. 48912.5)

The legislature provided direction to school officials by stating that suspensions and expulsions are not to be used as the primary means of student discipline. In this regard, Education Code section 48900.5 contains the following guideline: "Suspension shall be imposed only when other means of correction fail to bring about proper conduct." However, a student may be suspended for any of the reasons enumerated in section (a) through (e) of Section 48900 (items 1, 4, 9, 11, 12, and 15 in our list on pages 57-58), even upon a first offense, if the principal or superintendent determines that the student's presence on campus causes a danger to persons or property or threatens to disrupt the instructional process.

Suspensions by a Teacher

A teacher may suspend any student from his or her class when a student commits any of the fourteen acts set out in the law. A teacher's suspension is limited to the day of the suspension and the following day. The teacher is required to report the suspension immediately and send the pupil to the principal for appropriate action. In addition, the teacher is required to ask the parent or guardian of the student for a conference regarding the suspension (E.C. 48910).

If suspension by the teacher requires a student to remain at the school site, the school district is responsible for providing appropriate supervision. A student suspended from a class shall not be placed in another regular class during the period of suspension. However, if the pupil is assigned to more than one class per day, the student may be permitted to attend other classes.

In the case of suspension by a teacher, the student may not return to that class during the period of the suspension without concurrence of the teacher and principal. A teacher may require a suspended student to complete any assignments and tests missed during the suspension (E.C. 48913).

Suspension Procedures

Prior to student suspension the principal is required to complete the following procedures:

1. A principal or superintendent is required to conduct a conference. Whenever practicable, the teacher, supervisor, or school employee who referred the student should be present. At the conference, the pupil is to be informed of the reason for disciplinary action and the evidence against him or her. The student must also be given the opportunity to present his or her version and evidence in his or her defense (E.C. 48911). An exception to this requirement is possible when the principal determines that an emergency situation exists. An emergency situation is defined in section 48911 of the Education Code as "a clear and present danger to the life, safety, or health of pupils or school personnel."

2. At the time of the suspension, a school employee shall make a reasonable effort to contact the student's parent or guardian in person or by telephone. Whenever a student is suspended from school, the parent or guardian must be notified in writing of the suspension.

3. The suspension and its cause must be reported to the superintendent or the school board.

4. If the principal requests a parent conference, the parent or guardian shall respond to that request without delay. However, no penalties may be imposed on a student for failure of the student's parent or guardian to attend the conference.

5. In a case where expulsion of a student is being recommended, and the student's presence on campus constitutes a danger to persons or property or threatens disruption of the instructional process, the district may extend the suspension until the governing board has rendered a decision on the action. The parent must be notified in writing of the extended suspension.

Expulsions

Suspensions are of a limited nature; the student is still under the supervision of the parent and the school district. An expulsion, however, is defined as the separation of the student from the supervision of the school district. Expulsion is an action vested exclusively in the board of education. Unless authorized by state statute, school superintendents and principals do not have authority to expel a student.

Courts have held that expulsion of students from school jeopardizes a student's property interest in an education. Therefore, students who are considered for expulsion are guaranteed at least minimum due process under the Fourteenth Amendment.

Expellable Offenses

As discussed earlier, the specific acts for which students may be suspended from school are also violations that may result in expulsion from the district. The school board may expel students upon the first offense for causing physical injury to another person, possessing or selling weapons, possessing or selling illegal drugs, or committing robbery or extortion. However, the administrator must first determine that the pupil's presence on campus causes a danger to persons or property or threatens to disrupt the instructional process (E.C. 48900.5). The board may also expel a student who has damaged or stolen school property, possessed or used tobacco, committed an obscene act, had possession of drug paraphernalia, disrupted school activities, or received school property if the board finds that other means of correction are not feasible, or have repeatedly failed to bring about proper conduct, and that due to the nature of the violation, the presence of the pupil causes a continuing danger to the physical safety of the student or others (E.C. 48915).

Mandatory Recommendation for Expulsion

For some offenses a recommendation for expulsion by the principal or superintendent is mandatory. These offenses include:

1. causing serious physical injury to another person, except in self-defense
2. possession of any knife, explosive, or other dangerous object of no reasonable use to the pupil

3. unlawful possession of any controlled substance (except for a first offense involving sale of not more than one avoirdupois ounce of marijuana, other than concentrated cannabis)
4. robbery or extortion
5. assault or battery.

These offenses are listed in E.C. 48915. For these acts, the only possible exception to a mandatory recommendation for expulsion occurs if the principal or superintendent finds and reports in writing to the governing board that expulsion is inappropriate due to the circumstances.

The superintendent must recommend expulsion when a student is in possession of a firearm. Upon verification that a student knowingly possessed a firearm, the superintendent is required to immediately suspend the student and recommend expulsion. The student may not continue enrollment at a comprehensive secondary school or on the site where the offense took place (E.C. 48915).

Expulsion of Students with Exceptional Needs

In the case of a student enrolled in a special education program, the Education Code places several conditions on a governing board. These conditions, which must be satisfied prior to consideration of expulsion of a student enrolled in a special education program, are as follows:

1. The school or district is required to conduct an individualized education program (IEP) team meeting.

2. The IEP team must determine that the misconduct was not caused by, or was not a direct manifestation of, the pupil's identified disability.

3. The team must determine that the pupil had been appropriately placed at the time the misconduct occurred (E.C. 48915.5).

Provisions regarding students enrolled in special education are contained in Education Code sections 48915.5 and 48915.6.

The Expulsion Hearing

Education Code Section 48918 specifies the procedures for conducting expulsion hearings. The basic steps are enumerated below.

1. A hearing is required within thirty school days of the date the principal or superintendent determines that the pupil has committed any of the acts enumerated in Section 48900. A student and his parents are entitled, upon written request, to at least one postponement of the hearing for not more than thirty calendar days.

2. The pupil shall be entitled to a hearing to determine whether he or she shall be expelled. Written notice of the hearing shall be forwarded to the parent or guardian at least ten calendar days prior to the date of the hearing. The written notice shall contain the following information:

   a. the date and place of the hearing
   b. a statement of the specific facts and charges upon which the proposed expulsion is based
   c. a copy of the disciplinary rules of the district that relate to the alleged violation
   d. a notice to the student or the student's parent or guardian informing them of the right to appear in person or to be represented by counsel or a non-attorney advisor
   e. the right to inspect and obtain copies of all documents to be used at the hearing
   f. the right to confront and question all evidence presented
   g. the right to present oral and documentary evidence, including witnesses, on the student's behalf.

With respect to provision (f), the board, hearing officer, or administrative panel may, upon good cause, determine that the disclosure of the identity of a witness and the testimony of that witness would subject the witness to an unreasonable risk of harm. Upon this determination, the testimony of the witness may be presented at the hearing in the form of sworn declarations, which shall be examined only by the governing board, hearing officer, or administrative panel. Copies of these sworn declarations, edited to delete the name and identity of the witness, shall be made available to the offender.

3. The school board shall conduct the expulsion hearing in a session closed to the public, unless the pupil requests a public meeting.

4. An expulsion hearing may be conducted in three ways: by the board, by a hearing officer, or by an administrative panel.

5. Within three school days after the hearing, the hearing officer or administrative panel shall determine whether to recommend expulsion of the pupil. If the hearing officer or panel decides not to recommend expulsion, the student is reinstated and immediately permitted to return to school. If the hearing officer or panel recommends expulsion, findings of fact in support of the recommendation shall be prepared and submitted to the governing board.

6. The decision of the board to expel a student shall be based upon substantial evidence relevant to the charges presented at the expulsion hearing. Findings shall not be based solely upon hearsay evidence. Technical rules of evidence do not apply at an expulsion hearing. However, relevant evidence with probative effect is required.

7. A decision of the school board as to whether to expel a student shall be made within ten school days after the conclusion of the hearing. Under certain circumstances and for good cause the school board may extend the time period.

8. A record of the hearing shall be made. The record may be maintained by any means, including electronic recording, so long as a reasonably accurate and complete written transcription of the proceedings can be made.

9. Final action to expel a student can only be taken by the governing board, and this action must be taken in public session, although without stating the pupil's name. A decision of the governing board to expel shall be supported by substantial evidence showing that the pupil committed any of the acts enumerated in Education Code Section 48900.

10. Written notice of the decision to expel or to suspend the enforcement of an expulsion order shall be sent by the superintendent to the pupil or the pupil's parent or guardian. The written notice shall notify the parent or

guardian of the right to appeal the expulsion to the county board of education. The letter shall also notify the parent or guardian of his or her responsibility to inform a new school district of the expulsion.

The expulsion order and the causes shall be recorded in the pupil's mandatory interim record and shall be forwarded to any school in which the pupil subsequently enrolls upon receipt of a request from the admitting school for the pupil's school records. Provisions regarding an expelled student's eligibility to enroll in another program or district are contained in Education Code sections 48915.1 and 48915.2.

Summary

One can argue that public schools in America are in peril, and that survival in their present form is in serious jeopardy. Critics point out serious deficiencies in student academic achievement and the spiraling cost to the taxpayer of a free public education. However, the most serious threat to the schools is fear on the part of citizens, parents, and students that the neighborhood school is not a safe place for students. For the past several years, the Gallup Poll has reported that Americans rank lack of discipline as the number one problem facing the schools.

State legislatures, school boards, and the courts have reacted to this concern for the safety of students in a variety of ways. On the one hand, greater constitutional protection has been extended to students. For example, corporal punishment has been restricted in many states, and students have gained greater due process protection when school administrators consider suspension or expulsion.

However, at the same time, there has been a trend toward less tolerance on campus of students who are unruly, disruptive, or dangerous. The move toward "zero tolerance" has been a response to students bringing knives, guns, and other dangerous weapons onto campus. Many states, including California, are now mandating expulsion of students who bring weapons to school.

While unruly, disruptive students who actively present a threat to the general safety of students seem to be on the increase, the number of alternatives for dealing with these students remains essentially unchanged. A teacher has some options for controlling a difficult student: counseling, detention, working with a parent or guardian to improve citizenship, and limited power to suspend. A principal's authority is only slightly increased from that of a teacher: authority to suspend a student from school for a longer period of time or to recommend expulsion. The governing board has the ultimate power of expelling a student who has seriously defied school rules. The societal challenge of providing safe schools threatens to continue for some time.

Key Terms

1. California Administrative Code (Title 5)
2. California Education Code
3. corporal punishment
4. due process
5. expellable offenses
6. expulsion
7. expulsion hearing
8. expulsion of students with exceptional needs
9. *in loco parentis*
10. mandatory expulsion
11. property rights
12. suspendable offenses
13. suspension
14. zero tolerance

Discussion / Essay Questions

1. Within the past several years, student misconduct and violence have increased on school campuses. Discuss the major reasons for this increase.

2. The courts have granted teachers and principals power to control student conduct by the principle of *in loco parentis*. Define this principle and give examples of its use in public schools.

3. A teacher may suspend a student from his or her classroom. Discuss the procedures for and restrictions on suspension of a student by a teacher.

4. Suspensions and expulsions are becoming widely used by school districts to control student misconduct and violence on campus. What are the advantages and disadvantages of this means of attempting to control student behavior?

5. Seasoned teachers state that it is more difficult to gain cooperation in disciplining an unruly student that it once was. Do you agree or disagree with this statement? Support your conclusion with specific examples.

References

Batsche, G., & Knoff, H. (1994). Bullies and their victims: Understanding a pervasive problem in the schools. *School Psychology Review, 2*, 165-174.

Cauchon, D. (1999, April 13). Zero-tolerance policies lack flexibility. *USA Today*. Retrieved December 29, 2000 from the World Wide Web: http://www.usatoday. com/educate/ednews3.htm

Chancellor's Working Group on School-Based Violence Prevention. (1994, July). *Draft Report.* New York: New York City Board of Education.

de Vise, D. (1996, July 18). Law urged permitting expulsion of students for fake bomb threats. *San Diego Union*, p. A3.

Hudgins, H. C., & Vacca, R. S. (1985). *Law and education.* Charlottesville, VA: Michie.

Marshall, T. (1995, July 18). A world of pressures on parents, children. *Los Angeles Times*.

National Education Goals Panel. (1993). *The national education goals report*. Washington, DC: U.S. Government Printing Office.

National Institute of Education. (1978). *Violent schools—safe schools.* Washington, DC: U.S. Department of Health, Education and Welfare.

Pasternak, J. (1995, September 12). Student pays price for his disruptions. *Los Angeles Times,* p. A5.

Portner, J. (1995, April 19). Districts turn to expulsions to keep order. *Education Week.* Retrieved December 29, 2000 from the World Wide Web: http://www.edweek. org/ew/1995/30suspen.h14

Smith, F. L. (1994). Fighting back. *Executive Educator, 16* (10), 35-37.

U.S. juvenile crime growing swiftly, report warns. (1995, September 8). *Los Angeles Times*, p. A35.

Court Cases

Abella v. Riverside Unified School District, 135 Cal.Rptr. 177, 65 C.A.3d 153 (1976)

Bethel School District No. 403 v. Fraser, 478 U.S. 675, 106 S.Ct. 3159, 3164, 92 L.Ed.2d 549 (1986)

Goss v. Lopez, 419 U.S. 565, 95 S.Ct. 729, 42 L.Ed.2d 725 (1975)

Ingraham v. Wright, 430 U.S. 651 (1977)

Lovell v. Poway Unified School District, 847 F.Supp. 780, 784 (S.D. Cal., 1994)

Tinker v. Des Moines Independent Community School District, 393, U.S. 503, 506, 89 S.Ct. 733, 21 L.Ed.2d 731, 736 (1969)

Vernonia School District 47J v. Acton, 63 U.S.L.W. 4653 (U.S. June 26, 1995)

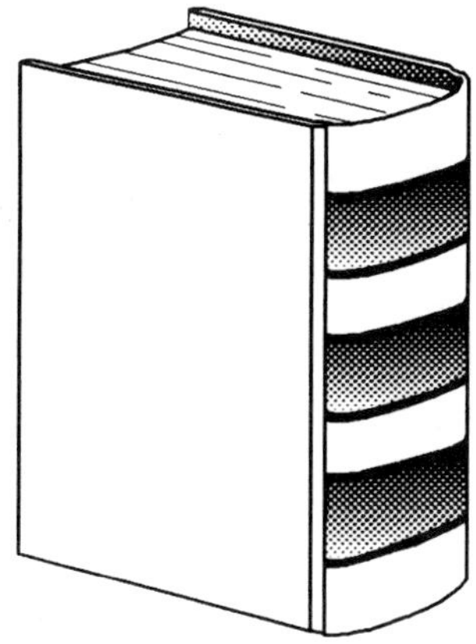

Chapter 5

Student Expression, the Constitution, and the Classroom

Introduction

High school students in a large high school in urban California pass through a metal detector each morning as they enter the school campus. When the local school board decided to install metal detectors, board members had received both support and resistance from the community. Speakers who lined up at school board meetings in support of the policy spoke about student safety. Those in opposition argued for student privacy. Support and opposition were about equally divided. However, as a result of an incident in 1999, support for metal detectors and other safety measures may be more strongly supported and student privacy a less persuasive argument in many American communities.

The incident referred to occurred on a June morning in 1999 at Columbine High School in Colorado. Two students, each dressed in a long black trench coat, opened rifle fire on their classmates and killed twelve fellow students. The "trenchcoat students," as they were referred to by the media, ran through the library and halls seeking to kill "athletic jocks" and black students. Columbine High School did not have a metal detector, but did employ a security officer who was aware of the background of these two students. Had the school installed metal detectors, would this tragedy have been avoided?

Although the Columbine shooting was ultimately regarded as an anomaly, it dramatically demonstrated the tension between student rights and the responsibility of school administrators and teachers to maintain a safe campus. Few issues have stirred as much passion among parents, state legislatures, and the courts. Over the past several decades, courts have faced the challenge of drawing boundaries between the Constitutional rights of individual students and the protection of the rights of the group. The guiding principle for establishing this balance has been the principle of *in loco parentis.* This concept is defined as the assumption of a parental role by teachers and administrators while children are under their jurisdiction.

What is the appropriate balance between students' freedom of expression and the rights of others in the education environment? If a teenage girl attends school with pink hair, jangly large nose rings, or a cropped shirt—or a male student comes in with a pierced tongue and green hair—do school personnel have the right to consider this appearance and attire inappropriate for a classroom setting? If a school official suspects that students are coming to school while under the influence of drugs, does that official have the right to require all students to submit to a drug test? Can the official search a student's backpack, locker, automobile, or pockets? May an administrator perform a strip search of a student?

School officials, state legislatures, and the courts have attempted to answer these questions. For example, the Supreme Court in *Vernonia School District vs. Acton* (1995) decreed that random urinalysis tests for drugs were legal.

Most cases of free expression involve student speech, student publications, or dress codes. Issues of student privacy include confidential student files and drug searches. This chapter addresses these issues, beginning with a brief historical discussion. Major court decisions are described. These issues remain controversial, so that continued societal discussion and new court cases may be expected.

Student Expression

Before the late 1960s, whenever a disagreement arose between school authorities and students, the courts usually sided with the school authorities. The primary criterion considered by the courts was whether the actions of a teacher or administrator had been reasonable. In the early 1970s several federal statutes were enacted that expanded the scope of student rights. A major concern of state legislatures was to give school officials sufficient authority to maintain safe campuses, while at the same time protecting student rights. Within the boundaries set by legislation, school administrators, too, struggle to maintain a proper balance between their obligation to maintain order and the rights of students to express themselves freely. Differences of opinion regarding application of the law frequently lead to court cases.

The past 40 years have seen the courts, as they interpret and apply the law, attempt to maintain the delicate balance between the Constitutionally guaranteed rights of individual students and the obligation of society to ensure a safe learning environment for young people. Whether the courts have succeeded depends upon the political viewpoint of the observer.

Throughout history the courts and schools have established a bond based upon the mutual obligations of teacher and student. The courts have long recognized that if schools are to function, the teacher must be able to exercise authority. To this end, the courts attempted to accord authority to a teacher much like that of a parent. The concept is referred to as *in loco parentis,* which means "in the place of the parent." This principle emanated from English law. Although courts have expanded the allowable extent of student expression, and concomitantly narrowed school authority, they have not deleted the notion of *in loco parentis*.

Constitutional Basis

The two Constitutional amendments that are most often cited in student expression cases are the First Amendment and the Fourth. Of all the freedoms guaranteed in this country, none is more protected than freedom of speech and the press and the right to peaceable assembly as established in the First Amendment, which states:

> Congress shall make no law respecting an establishment of religion, or prohibiting the free exercise thereof; or abridging the freedom of speech, or of the press, or the right of the people peaceably to assemble, and to petition the Government for a redress of grievances.

The Fourth Amendment reads:

> The right of the people to be secure in their persons, houses, papers, and effects, against unreasonable searches and seizures, shall not be violated, and no Warrants shall issue, but upon probable cause, supported by oath or affirmation, and particularly describing the place to be searched, and the persons or things to be seized.

In addition to these two amendments, several landmark cases provide boundaries and guidelines for student expression. A major issue addressed by the courts in these cases is "reasonableness." This term is not limited to Constitutional issues. Indeed, whenever judges are confronted with sticky issues of tort law, the meaning of "reasonableness" comes into play. Its legal definition calls for behavior that is proper, rational, and fair, while rejecting behavior that is excessive or inappropriate.

Tinker v. Des Moines

The pros and cons of free speech were hotly debated during the 1960s. At that time the daily news revolved around the Vietnam War and free speech on college campuses. Many riots occurred, with university students storming administrative offices and remaining for days. Many students were injured and some were killed during these confrontations. Soon, issues of free speech were no longer confined to colleges, but filtered down the grades in schools throughout the country.

During this period of national turmoil, the Supreme Court attempted to resolve the issue of student free expression. The key case was *Tinker v. Des Moines Independent Community School District* (1969).

Petitioner John F. Tinker, 15 years old, and petitioner Christopher Eckhardt, 16, attended high schools in Des Moines, Iowa. Petitioner Mary Beth Tinker, John's sister, was a 13-year-old student in junior high school. The incident that gave rise to the suit was triggered by a meeting of adults and young people in December of 1965 at the Eckhardt home. The participants discussed how to publicize their objections to the Vietnam War. It was decided they would wear black armbands during the holiday season.

After hearing of the plan, the principals of the Des Moines schools met and developed a policy that any student wearing an armband to school would be asked to remove it. A student who refused would be suspended until he or she returned without the armband. It is interesting to note that only a few of the 18,000 district students wore armbands. Some students made angry remarks to those who were wearing armbands, but there were no fights or threats of violence.

On December 16, 1965, Mary Beth and Christopher decided to wear the armbands to school. The next day, John Tinker wore his armband. The three students were suspended from school and sent home until they would come back without the armbands.

A complaint was filed in the United States District Court by the fathers of the students under section 1983 of Title 42 of the United States Code. The key issue was whether wearing of insignia or other markings in school was a Constitutionally protected right. After hearing the evidence, the court invalidated the rule prohibiting students from wearing black armbands as a protest against the war. The court stated that "undifferentiated fear or apprehension of disturbance is not enough to overcome the right to freedom of expression." The court declared that the administration could prohibit the wearing of symbols only if such activity would "materially and substantially disrupt the work and discipline of the school." The Supreme Court emphasized that educators have the authority and duty to maintain discipline in schools, but that, as they exert control, they must also consider students' Constitutional rights.

Justice Fortas presented the opinion of the Court. The Court majority decided there was no evidence that the wearing of armbands would substantially interfere with the work of the school or impinge upon the rights of other students. Often quoted from the decision is the sentence, "It can hardly be argued that either students or teachers shed their Constitutional rights to freedom of speech or expression at the schoolhouse gate."

The Court was not unanimous in its decision. The minority opinion was written by Justice Black, who demurred from the majority decision because he did not want the schools to serve as a platform for the exercise of free speech. Justice Black pointed out that the armbands did cause comment in the schools. He felt that the display had taken the minds of students off their schoolwork and diverted it to thoughts about the Vietnam War. He felt that this decision could harbor a new revolutionary period in the nation's history.

Justice Black's comments are of interest because they demonstrate that the *Tinker* decision was debatable. It conveyed the view that courts should not be involved in running a school. In keeping with that position, subsequent cases have provided school administrators with seemingly broad authority to regulate student speech. A 1986 decision of the Supreme Court illustrates how the Court views a student's lewd speech in a school assembly.

Bethel School District No. 403 v. Fraser

As summarized by U.S. Supreme Court Chief Justice Burger, the case arose from a speech by Matthew Fraser, a student at Bethel High School in Bethel, Washington, on April 26, 1983. In his speech, nominating another student for student government, Matthew "referred to his candidate in terms of an elaborate, graphic, and explicit sexual metaphor." The comments may seem mild by current standards; for example, Matthew remarked, "I know a man who is firm—he's firm in his pants, he's firm in his shirt, his character is firm—but most . . . of all, his belief in you, the students of Bethel, is firm." At the time, some students were embarrassed by the speech, while others applauded.

The Assistant Principal called Matthew into her office the next morning and informed him that the school considered his speech a violation of policy and that he would be suspended and removed as a graduation speaker. Matthew's father brought action in the courts and alleged that the speech was indistinguishable from the armband protest in the *Tinker* case.

The U.S. District Court held that the school's actions violated Matthew's right to freedom of speech, that the school's discipline rules were unconstitutionally vague, and that the student's removal from the graduation speaker's list violated the due process clause. The court awarded Matthew $278 in damages and $12,750 in litigation costs and attorney fees.

In the meantime, Matthew had been elected graduation speaker by a write-in vote of his classmates and gave the graduation speech. In 1985 the Ninth Circuit Court of Appeals affirmed the judgment of the district court.

Then, in 1986, the U.S. Supreme Court reversed the decision of the Ninth Circuit Court and found in favor of the school district. The Court held that the discipline imposed upon Matthew did not violate his First Amendment rights. The Court differentiated the *Bethel* case from *Tinker* on two grounds: first, the plaintiff in *Bethel* did not espouse a particular political point of view, as did those in *Tinker*; second, *Bethel* did involve a substantial disruption of the school environment in that this particular speech was damaging, especially to a less mature audience.

The Court considered the fundamental values of "habits and manners of civility." The sensibilities of fellow students were considered. The language of the speech, while acceptable in a gathering of adults, was not acceptable or permitted in front of children in a public school. Matthew's remarks were also considered offensive to female students because his comments glorified male sexuality and were acutely insulting to teenage girls.

Many courts followed the *Bethel* decision in granting more rights to school administrators. Thus, *Bethel* came to allow school authorities considerable latitude in censoring lewd and vulgar student expression. The Court held that it is a responsibility of a school to protect its captive student audience from exposure to lewd, vulgar, and offensive speech. In cases where students belittled school administrators, the courts also found for the administrators, stating that a certain amount of decorum is necessary in schools to maintain the educational process. *Bethel* stands as a major case in determining the appropriate balance between students' Constitutional rights and the duty of public school officials to maintain an appropriate and safe environment for learning.

Student Publications

Are there limitations on what students may publish? Do they have the same freedoms as adults under the First Amendment? Some of the most hotly debated cases in the schools have dealt with student publications.

Clearly, the Constitution protects the right of adults to a free press. In fact, it was the intent of the founding fathers to enable the press to censure the government, if needed. It was also understood that the press would endeavor to be truthful and to publish material without malice or intent to malign. However, courts view private and public individuals differently. Public individuals generally have a harder time obtaining a favorable judgement in a libel action (Yudof, 1991).

Similarly, freedom of the press in public schools is governed by a different set of rules from those that pertain to newspapers for the public at large. The courts have typically ruled that a valid educational purpose must be served by student publications. On the other hand, school officials do not have *carte blanche* to censor student newspapers. Of additional concern to the courts is that rules governing student publications are uniformly enforced.

Hazelwood School District v. Kuhlmeier

Each court decision must consider a unique set of circumstances. *Hazelwood School District v. Kuhlmeier* (1988) demonstrates the Court's interpretation of the First Amendment in combination with the importance of maintaining an educational purpose. We note that *Hazelwood* is unusual in that a decision of the U.S. Supreme Court is not the "last word" for California. First we examine the Supreme Court decision.

Hazelwood reviewed the extent of editorial control of a student newspaper by school officials. The petitioners on appeal were school officials from the Hazelwood School District in St. Louis County, Missouri. Respondents were three former Hazelwood students. The students had been staff members of the school newspaper, *Spectrum*. In the original suit, the students charged that school officials had violated their First Amendment rights by deleting two pages of articles from the May 13, 1983, issue.

Spectrum was written and edited by the Journalism II class at Hazelwood. During most of the 1982-83 school year, the course had been taught by Robert Stergos. The newspaper had been published every three weeks, with 4,500 copies distributed to students, school personnel, and members of the community. Stergos left Hazelwood to take a job in private industry on April 29, 1983, when the May 13 edition of *Spectrum* was nearing completion. At that time appellant Emerson took Stergos's place as newspaper adviser for the remaining weeks of the term.

Typically, the journalism teacher would submit proofs of each *Spectrum* issue to Principal Reynolds for his review prior to publication. On May 10, Emerson delivered the proofs of the May 13 edition to Reynolds, who objected to two of the articles scheduled to appear in that edition. One of the stories described three Hazelwood students' experiences with pregnancy; the other discussed the impact of divorce on students at the school. The students who wrote the articles brought suit because the articles about pregnancy and divorce were omitted from the final copy.

The U.S. Supreme Court found that the administration at Hazelwood had not violated the students' First Amendment rights. This opinion gives educators the power to exercise editorial control over the style and content of student speech in school-sponsored expressive activities, as long as their actions are reasonably related to legitimate pedagogical concerns. Moreover, school authorities can control the time, place, and manner of the distribution of a student newspaper. Publications paid for with school funds or produced as part of the curriculum (for example, in a journalism class) are subject to more controls than are student school newspapers published off campus.

Now we turn to the application of *Hazelwood* in California. According to Romero and Huguenin (1988), staff attorneys for the California Teachers' Association, the *Hazelwood* decision is more restrictive of student rights than section 48907 in the California Education Code. That code directs public school personnel to allow student expression unless it is "obscene, libelous, or slanderous" or threatens to incite students to "commission of unlawful acts on school premises or the violation of lawful school regulations or the substantial disruption of the orderly operation of the school." This restriction specifically includes school publications, bulletin boards, and such expressions as petitions and badges. It further requires school personnel to show that the material falls into the prohibited categories of section 48907 before, not after, suppressing the publication or other expression. Romero and Huguenin conclude that section 48907 "would probably survive any specific challenge to it because of current California Supreme Court precedent." It appears, then, that the role of the U.S. Supreme Court is to ensure that citizens have *at least* the freedoms guaranteed by the Constitution, specifically the Bill of Rights, but that a state may enact legislation that sets a broader definition.

Search, Seizure, and Drug Testing

School administrators are frequently confronted with the decision whether or not to search a student's desk, locker, pockets, purse, book bag, coat, shoes and socks, or automobile. On the one hand, an administrator is charged to maintain order and discipline on campus and to protect the health and welfare of all students. On the other hand, this necessity must be balanced against the protected privacy rights of students. The Fourth Amendment and several court cases provide guidance in answering this question.

The Fourth Amendment of the United States Constitution, quoted earlier, guarantees citizens the right "to be secure in their persons, houses, papers and effects, against unreasonable searches and seizures." To support this right, "no warrants shall issue, but upon probable cause."

The Fourth Amendment includes five important components. First an individual's control over his or her person and property is emphasized: "persons, houses, papers, and effects." Second, "unreasonable searches and seizures" are forbidden. Third, a search cannot be instituted without probable cause or evidence that a search is necessary. Fourth, a warrant must be specific, describing the place to be searched and the articles to be seized. Last, a magistrate or judge is interposed between the individual and the government, requiring that the government justify the necessity of the search.

Three of these five components are applicable to a student search. Students have a right to privacy in their person and property, they are protected from unreasonable seizures and searches, and a search must be specific as to what is sought and where. Although school officials need not provide evidence of probable cause or obtain a search warrant from a judge, they must have "reasonable suspicion" as a basis for a search.

New Jersey v. T.L.O.

The prevailing case regarding school searches and seizures is *New Jersey v. T.L.O.* (1985). This case clearly upheld the principle of *in loco parentis.*

On March 7, 1980, a teacher at Piscataway High School in Middlesex County, New Jersey, discovered two girls smoking in a lavatory. One of the girls was T.L.O., who at the time was a 14-year-old high school freshman. Because smoking in the lavatory violated a school rule, the two girls were taken to the principal's office. T.L.O. denied that she had been smoking at all. A subsequent search of her purse revealed a pack of cigarettes, cigarette rolling papers, a small amount of marijuana, a pipe, an index card of names of students who appeared to owe money to T.L.O., and a quantity of one dollar bills.

T.L.O. was then turned over to her mother, who took her to a police station, where she ultimately confessed to selling marijuana. On the basis of the confession and the evidence, the state brought delinquency charges against T.L.O. in the Juvenile and Domestic Relations Court of Middlesex County. T.L.O., contending that the administrator's search of her purse violated the Fourth Amendment, moved to suppress the evidence found in her purse.

The Supreme Court upheld the right of the school to conduct the search, holding that as long as a school official "has reasonable grounds to believe that the student possesses evidence of illegal activity or activity that would interfere with school discipline and order," the search was legal. The Court upheld the *in loco parentis* doctrine by considering the Fourth Amendment search and seizure restrictions while also recognizing the necessity of reasonable action to promote student learning and safety.

The Court indicated that the Fourth Amendment is applicable in school situations, but that reasonableness must prevail if a search is to be Constitutionally valid. A major consideration of the Court was whether a teacher or administrator gives consideration to "reasonableness" when a search is initiated. To be judged reasonable, a search must have been pointed to by the factors leading up to it. For example, prior to the search, had a school administrator observed that the student appeared to be under the influence of drugs? Or had the administrator been informed that drugs were in the student's locker? The more intensive the search, the stronger must be the basis for suspicion. However, individual privacy is still observed in most cases, even intrusive drug searches.

Canine Searches

Canine searches predate the *New Jersey v. T.L.O.* case. The Tenth Circuit Court of Appeals in *Zamora v. Pomeroy* (1981) upheld the use of dogs in the exploratory sniffing of lockers. The court noted that since the schools gave notice at the beginning of the year that the lockers might be periodically opened, the lockers were jointly possessed by both student and school. The Seventh Circuit Court in *Doe v. Renfrow* (1980) ruled that school officials stood *in loco parentis* and had the right to use dogs to seek out drugs. The court affirmed that school officials had a duty to maintain an educational environment that was conducive to learning.

In a federal district court case, *Jones v. Latexo Independent School District* (1980), the decision did not conform with *Doe* and *Zamora*. In this case the district used dogs to sniff both students and automobiles. The court ruled that in the absence of individual suspicion, having the dogs sniff the students was unreasonable and intrusive. Moreover, since the students could not go to their cars during the school day, sniffing the vehicles was also unreasonable.

The use of drug-sniffing dogs on a school campus was challenged in a California case (*B.C. v. Plumas*) in 1999. The Plumas Unified School District, concerned with possible possession of drugs, asked the sheriff to bring a drug-sniffing dog to the campus. Students were required to walk by a deputy sheriff and his dog. The dog alerted on the same student twice; however, when the student was searched, no drugs were found.

A classmate of the student who was searched, "B.C.," sued in federal court, alleging that he had been deprived of his Fourth Amendment right to be free from unreasonable search. The Ninth Circuit Court of Appeals ruled that the school had the right to sniff students' belongings, but—except in case of reasonable suspicion of drug possession—not their person. In response, the District Attorney of Alameda County posted on the Internet the view (District Attorney, n.d.) that the court opinion was "logically and legally unsound" and encouraging law enforcement officers to continue use of drug-sniffing dogs "so long as [there is no] physical contact with a person for whom reasonable suspicion or probable cause does not exist." This posting further noted that "decisions of the U.S. Court of Appeals interpreting federal law are not binding on California courts."

Turning from law to policy, many high schools have eliminated student lockers for fear that drugs or weapons might be kept there. While this action may protect students from drugs or weapons, the downside is that many secondary students carry 40 to 60 pounds of books around with them all day.

Vernonia School District v. Acton

A 1995 decision of the Supreme Court illustrates how a seeming precedent may fail to establish a foundation for later decisions. In *Vernonia v. Acton* (1995), the Court chose to part with precedent by validating Vernonia School District's policy of "suspicionless" drug testing of student athletes. Few cases regarding drug searches have had such an effect as *Vernonia vs. Acton*. The Supreme Court found for the district and its right to conduct random drug searches of student athletes with*out* suspicion. The Court "balanced away" the Fourth Amendment protection of students when it classified the district's search as reasonable under the circumstances.

In 1991 James Acton tried out for the football team in Vernonia School District, Oregon. James was twelve years old and in the seventh grade. At practice, all of the students were given a drug testing consent form by the coach. James took the form home and discussed it with his parents. They decided that James would not sign the form. As a result, James was declared ineligible for school sports until he would sign.

James's parents filed suit on his behalf in the United States District Court for the District of Oregon (Samay, 1997). The Actons requested declaratory judgement and injunctive relief based upon their belief that the district's policy interfered with their son's rights under the Fourth Amendment and Article I, Section 9, of the Oregon Constitution. The U.S. District Court denied their petition for relief, and the Actons appealed. Reversing the District Court decision, the United States Court of Appeals for the Ninth Circuit held that the district's need to randomly search its students did not outweigh the privacy interests of student athletes.

However, recognizing the importance of the issue, the United States Supreme Court granted a petition (writ of certiorari) to determine whether random urinalysis drug testing of students who participated in Vernonia's athletic programs violated the Fourth and Fourteenth Amendments to the United States Constitution. In 1995 the U.S. Supreme Court, by a 6-3 decision, reversed the lower courts and found that the district's policy conformed with the Fourth and Fourteenth Amendments. The urine test was legitimate on the ground that governmental interest outweighs a student's privacy rights. The court found that athletes are subject to reduced privacy rights in that they have special grade and citizenship requirements as well as required medical examinations. It was also noted that athletes participate in communal undressing and showering. All these conditions reduce the claim of physical privacy.

Why did this case cause such a "stir" among students? In this decision, the Supreme Court determined that random urinalysis tests of student athletes, without reasonable suspicion, could be characterized as reasonable. Clearly, this important case will continue to serve as a precedent.

Student Dress Codes and Uniforms

As students have sought to express their individuality in clothing, hairstyles, and ornamentation, school administrators have become concerned over possible distraction from, even disruption of, the learning environment. At times these have led to suspension from school. In California, state law specifically allows adoption of dress codes (E.C. 35183, 35294). Schoolwide uniforms, heretofore a common practice in private schools, are also mentioned (E.C. 35183). Such issues have elicited highly emotional responses and have given rise to a number of lawsuits.

Many public school students and parents are opposed to any student dress code. They believe that a student should maintain his or her individuality by wearing whatever is desired. The courts, on the other hand, have generally supported a district's authority to regulate student dress and personal appearance—if the dress or appearance becomes so extreme as to interfere with a school's learning atmosphere. The *Tinker* decision established the precedent for students' right to wear passive symbols to convey a message that is Constitutionally protected. However, the *Tinker* decision noted that even passive symbols can become disruptive in some circumstances (Valente, 1998).

Beyond the question of a school dress code is the growing popularity of school uniforms. California's Long Beach Unified School District, for example, received nationwide attention when it introduced school uniforms. The district reports that since 1994, when the policy was introduced, the uniform dress code helped reduce violent crime in the district. The number of school fights was reduced by half. The district also reports fewer school suspensions, and the introduction of the dress code is given some credit for this achievement (Kennedy, 1995). It is too early to predict, but Long Beach's success may spread to other districts and states. New York, Virginia, Georgia, Louisiana and Maryland have passed laws authorizing school districts to order their students into uniform.

Student Records

The Supreme Court has recognized that the Constitution protects student privacy. Students have the right to expect the school to keep confidential any personal information about themselves. However, this right has limits. School employees who, in the course of fulfilling their duties, have a legitimate need for information about a student may access confidential records.

Parents and guardians, too, have rights. The right to view educational records includes all records directly related to the student. Records, by definition, may be written, on film, on tape, in computers, or any other form. A school must respond to a request to view records within a reasonable time, 45 days being the maximum.

In *Fay v. South Colonie Central School District* (1986) the Second Circuit Court awarded damages to a parent who brought action against the district for refusal to provide records under the Family Education Rights and Privacy Act (20 U.S.C. 1232g [1982]). The plaintiff had joint legal custody of two minor children and requested to have report cards sent to him. School officials refused his request. The court felt that this refusal clearly violated the rights of the parent.

Legal challenges to school record keeping procedures have sometimes resulted in court orders to school administrators to expunge irrelevant information from students' permanent folders. In some situations, students have successfully brought libel suits against school authorities who allegedly recorded and communicated defamatory information about them.

Summary

School administrators can expect continuing involvement in resolving conflicts between the rights of students and the need to maintain safe settings for learning. In addition, state legislatures, the Congress, and the courts will confront issues in this arena. Some of the questions to be kept in mind include:

- What are the rights of students and employees on a school campus?
- How does one guard against violating a student's Constitutional rights?
- What is "reasonable suspicion"?
- Under what circumstances may a student's locker, clothing, or automobile be searched?
- May districts install metal detectors at the entrances and exits of each campus?

Perhaps the single most important principle for the school official to keep in mind is that students do have rights. As a consequence, the school leader must maintain a balance between the rights of the individual and the right of all the students to a safe and educationally sound school environment. Where to draw the line is an important choice about which reasonable people may differ.

Issues of free speech, student right of publication, and student search will continue to surface and to change, in part due to the membership of the Supreme Court at any given time. Recent case law related to student expression shows growing deference to principals and other administrators. However, it is always important to keep abreast of the latest legislation and court rulings. In addition, wise school administrators develop clearly written, educationally sound policies that are communicated to students and parents on a regular basis.

Key Terms

1. canine search
2. First Amendment rights
3. Fourth Amendment rights
4. Eighth Amendment rights
5. *in loco parentis*
6. metal detectors
7. reasonable suspicion
8. reasonableness
9. suspicionless drug testing

Discussion / Essay Questions

1. If asked to explain why you had asked a student to empty her purse, how would you describe "reasonable suspicion"?

2. Assume you are the adviser to a school newspaper at the secondary level. What types of subject matter might you edit out of the newspaper? What not? Why do you believe that you are on sound legal grounds to delete the material you have described?

3. What recommendations do you have on whether and how to structure Internet communications among students at the secondary level?

4. What is the impact of the *Vernonia School Board vs. Acton* case on the actions of school administrators? Do you feel that a urinalysis test given randomly is justified—or invasive and uncalled for? Why?

References

District Attorney Point of View Online; *B.C. v. Plumas Unified School District et al.* (no date). Alameda County, CA: District Attorney's Office. Retrieved from the World Wide Web: http://www.co.alameda.ca.us/da/pov/bc.shtml

Kennedy, M. J. (1995, August 19). A fashion statement with real meaning. *Los Angeles Times.*

Romero, R., & Huguenin, E., Jr. (1988, March). Respecting student First Amendment rights. *CTA Action*, Legal Issues section.

Samay, C. E. (1997). Judicial activisim works the Constitution out of shape—*Acton* and its atrophic effect on the Fourth Amendment rights of student athletes. pp. 291-314.

Valente, W. D. (1998). *Law in the schools* (4th ed.). New York: Merrill.

Yudof, M. G. (1991). *Educational policy and the law*. Belmont, CA: Wadsworth.

Court Cases

B.C. v. Plumas Unified School District, 192 F.3d 1260 (9th Cir. 1999)

Bethel School District No. 403 v. Frasier, 478 U.S. 675, 106 S.Ct. 3159 (1986)

Doe v. Renfrow, 631 F.2d 91 (7th Cir. 1980)

Fay v. South Colonie Central School District, 802 F. 2d 21 (2nd Cir. 1986)

Hazelwood School District v. Kuhlmeier, 484 U.S. 260, 108 S.Ct. 562 (1988)

Jones v. Latexo Independent School District, 499 F.Supp. 223 (E.D.Tex. 1980)

New Jersey v. T.L.O., S.Ct. 1985, 469 U.S. 325, 105 S.Ct. 733 (1985)

Tinker v. Des Moines Independent Community School District, 393 U.S. 503, 89 S.Ct. 733, 21 L.Ed. 2nd 731 (1969), 796F (9th Cir.), 115 S.Ct. (1993)

Vernonia School District 47J v. Acton, 515 U.S. 646, 115 S.Ct. 2386, 132 L.Ed.2d 564 (1995).

Zamora v. Pomeroy, 639 F.2d 662 (10th Cir. 1981)

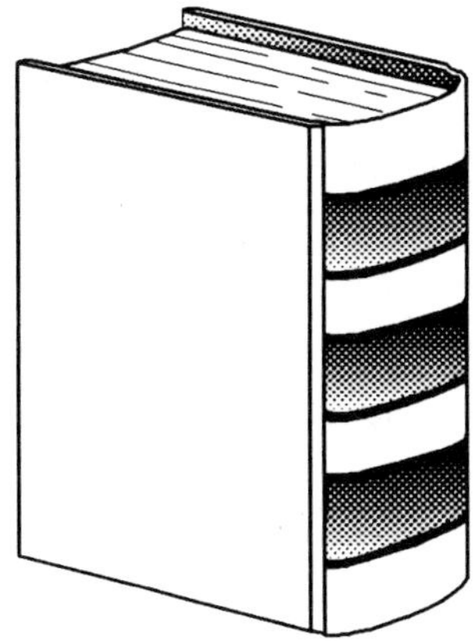

Chapter 6

Special Education and the Law

Introduction

A seventh-grade special education student, Philadelfio Armijo of New Mexico, was found by his parents in his bedroom, having shot himself to death. He killed himself after several altercations at school, in connection with which he was suspended. A counselor drove him home and dropped him off without contacting the parents, who filed suit in the U.S. District Court in March of 1996. The plaintiffs claimed that defendants—the district, its board and superintendent, the principal, counselor, and an aide to whom the boy had several times remarked that he might be better off dead—had violated the Individuals with Disabilities Education Act. They further argued that the district, board, and superintendent should have trained staff members to handle potentially violent and suicidal students. Finally, they alleged that defendant school personnel had violated their son's Fourteenth Amendment rights: first, by creating a danger for the boy, and second, by having established a special relationship with their son that created an exceptional responsibility to guard him from harm (Zirkel, 1999).

This case, *Armijo v. Wagon Mount Public Schools* (1998), illustrates the challenges involved in working with students with disabilities, especially in case of violence or discipline problems. On the one hand, board policies of zero tolerance for violence and drugs require that the student be excluded from school. On the other hand, the pupil's misbehavior must be shown unrelated to his or her disability; otherwise, the student may not be excluded.

On appeal, the Tenth Circuit Court concluded that it lacked jurisdiction with respect to the first two issues, which the district court had found untenable. With respect to the "danger creation" theory, the Circuit Court acted to dismiss the complaint against the aide, but indicated that the administrator and counselor may have been responsible. The higher court decided that none of the school organizations or personnel had established a special relationship. However, the case was remanded to the district court for trial as to liability for the suicide on the part of the principal or counselor. As soon as the counselor, as directed by the principal, drove the student home and left him there, the district and administrator had become legally at risk.

It is crucial that school leaders know the laws governing the education of students with disabilities. The issues involved in serving the needs of all students while attending to those with special needs are truly complex. In addition, the legal risks are increased by the number and power of parent advocacy groups. This chapter outlines the historical development of federal and state legislation that requires states and school districts to provide for the education of handicapped children. Special education terminology, the requirements of special education programs, and important court cases are reviewed.

Special Education Terms

Because of the highly specialized nature of the language of special education, some of the more common terms are defined here.

Assessment: All districts are responsible for identifying and serving students with exceptional needs. Once an individual has been identified and screened as potentially in need of special services, the pupil is formally assessed. A multi-disciplinary team administers a range of tests and utilizes diagnostic materials to determine specific areas of educational need. However, a pupil is not placed in a special education program if the observed difficulties are due solely to unfamiliarity with English; temporary physical disability; social maladjustment; or environmental, cultural, or economic factors.

Free and Appropriate Public Education (FAPE): The phrase "free and appropriate public education" had its origin in case law of the 1970s that declared education free and available to all citizens.

Inclusion: "Inclusion" has largely replaced the term "mainstreaming" and indicates placement of students with disabilities within the general education classroom. The premise underlying this practice is that disabled students can best be served in a classroom where the regular teacher's instruction is supplemented by support personnel and services. The fundamental belief underlying inclusion is that all students, both disabled and non-disabled, will benefit from being educated together in the same setting.

Individualized Educational Program (IEP): The IEP is a plan—including goals, objectives, evaluation, and measurement criteria—to address the needs of a student with disabilities.

Least Restrictive Environment (LRE): The terms "least restrictive environment," "mainstreaming," and "inclusion" are used interchangeably, although they do not mean quite the same thing. "Least restrictive environment" emerged from the Individuals with Disabilities Education Act, which requires that students with disabilities be educated to the maximum extent appropriate with peers without disabilities.

Mainstreaming: This practice allows students with learning disabilities to participate in the regular educational program to the fullest extent possible, as written into the IEP. Mainstreaming may occur in academic and/or social areas.

Special Education Local Planning Area (SELPA): Special education may be provided by a single school district or by a group of districts. A district or group may also furnish special education services in cooperation with the county office of education. The combination of services by several school districts and the county office of education is referred to as Special Education Local Planning Area. Usually, governance of the program is left to the local entity that provides services to special education students.

Historical Context of Special Education

In the 1800s children with special needs were dubbed "idiot" and "insane." Prior to the 1970s, it was not uncommon that children with special needs either were placed in special schools or did not attend school at all (Yell, 1998). The goal of a free, appropriate education for students with disabilities has been largely achieved through pressure from parent advocacy groups, legislative action, and legal precedents as a result of Supreme Court decisions. Three major cases advanced the educational rights of students with disabilities. The cases were *Brown v. Board of Education* (1954), *Pennsylvania Association for Retarded Citizens v. Commonwealth of Pennsylvania* (1972), and *Mills v. Board of Education* (1972).

Brown v. Board of Education of Topeka

Prior to the enactment of federal laws concerning students with disabilities, only the Fourteenth Amendment and state statutes addressed the needs of these young people (McCarthy, Cambron-McCabe, & Thomas, 1998). Special education was brought to the legislative agenda as an indirect result of the equality of opportunity movement in the 1950s and 1960s, which resulted in the landmark case *Brown v. Board of Education* (1954). Although the 1954 *Brown* decision dealt with racial segregation, rather than special education, the Court's conclusion that education must be available to all children on equal terms was later extended to include children with disabilities.

The central theme of the *Brown* decision, and one that would provide the underpinning to the movement for inclusion, was the Constitutional guarantee of equal protection under the law as stipulated under the Fourteenth Amendment. The decision reads, in part:

> No State shall make or enforce any law which shall abridge the privileges or immunities of citizens of the United States; nor shall any State deprive any person of life, liberty, or property, without due process of law; nor deny to any person within its jurisdiction the equal protection of the laws.

The *Brown* decision ultimately extended this guarantee to require that each state provide a free public education for all its citizens. This decision led the way to two hallmark decisions challenging state statutes that excluded students with disabilities from school. These two decisions were *Pennsylvania Association for Retarded Citizens v. Commonwealth of Pennsylvania* and *Mills v. Board of Education of the District of Columbia*, both rendered in 1972.

Pennsylvania Association for Retarded Citizens v. Commonwealth of Pennsylvania

This Pennsylvania (PARC) case was the first major suit brought by parents of students with disabilities. It named as defendants school districts, the Pennsylvania Board of Education, and the secretaries of Education and Public Welfare. The plaintiffs argued that children with mental retardation were not receiving a publicly supported education. The plaintiffs contended that students' rights were violated under the Fourteenth Amendment. They brought forth four important points:

- All children with mental disabilities can benefit from training and education.
- The outcomes of public education are not limited to book-learning; rather, learning to feed and clothe oneself can qualify as an academic experience.
- Since Pennsylvania offered a free public education, students with disabilities should also receive this benefit.
- Mentally disabled children who are exposed to education at an early age show higher gains overall than those who begin education at a later age.

The advocates in the PARC case scored a major victory that set the stage for continued improvements in educational programs for students with disabilities. A consent agreement was negotiated providing that all students between the ages of 6 and 21 would receive free public education. An additional clause expedited inclusion of disabled students into the regular education program. This clause required that programs for those students with mental retardation must be very similar to programs for those without disabilities.

Mills v. Board of Education

The other half of the pair of court decisions that influenced the direction of education for students with disabilities was the *Mills* case. This case was initiated in the District of Columbia for all out-of-school students with disabilities. Guardians and parents of seven children brought the suit. These seven children represented a variety of disabilities including mental retardation, epilepsy, hyperactivity, and physical disability.

The court judgement was handed down in favor of the students. The school board was directed to provide all students with disabilities a free public education. However, the most important part of this decision was institution of procedural safeguards. These safeguards include written procedures for due process, the right to appeal decisions, and access to records. In addition, the court determined that no child with a disability could be excluded on the basis of insufficient resources in a school district and, further, that each child must be individually assessed and placed in a publicly supported program suited to the child's needs. The term "least restrictive environment" originated with this case, the court stating that a child should be placed in the least restrictive environment in which he or she can function.

After these two cases were settled, the stage was set for many more cases regarding students with disabilities. They were indeed harbingers of favorable times for parents of students with disabilities. However, laws that were enacted as a result of this trend resulted in inconsistent practices. It became increasingly clear to educators and parents that some type of federal intervention was necessary.

Federal Legislation and *Rowley*

Although several key pieces of legislation related to students with disabilities have been enacted by Congress from 1973 to the present, four of these have had direct impact upon educational opportunities for children with special needs. In addition, a 1982 U.S. Supreme Court decision further clarified the phrase "free and appropriate public education."

Public Law 93-112: Vocational Rehabilitation

As a result of the previously discussed court cases, Congress enacted federal legislation designed to eliminate discrimination against disabled students. The first instance was approved in 1973 as Public Law 93-112, the Vocational Rehabilitation Act. This law forbade discrimination on the basis of an individual's handicap in any program or activity that received federal assistance. The act also defined "handicapped" and charged schools to locate all people who might qualify for special assistance. The law further required the schools to provide these individuals with a free and appropriate public education.

Public Law 94-142: Education for All Handicapped

Public Law 93-112 was followed by Public Law 94-142, the Education for All Handicapped Children Act, approved by Congress in 1975. This law, referred to as EAHCA, required all states to establish a free and appropriate educational program for students with special educational needs. It also established procedural safeguards around the individualized educational program (IEP) required for each child. While this legislation has greatly benefitted children in need of special programs, it has at the same time had some negative effects on schools. For example, it has produced as much, if not more, litigation than any other federal education statute on the books.

Public Law 101-476: Individuals with Disabilities Education Act

In 1990 Congress renamed EAHCA the "Individuals with Disabilities Education Act" (IDEA). This legislation, P.L. 101-476, replaced the term "handicapped" with "disabled," so that "handicapped children" were referred to as "children with disabilities." IDEA broadly defined disabilities to include mental retardation, visual and hearing impairments, serious emotional disturbance, autism, orthopedic impairment, traumatic brain injury, and other health impairments or specific learning disabilities. Students in late stages of AIDS fall within the above coverage, but the laws are not fully developed on the point at which an AIDS condition becomes sufficiently disabling to qualify for IDEA benefits.

The act directed states and school districts to include disabled students in regular education programs whenever possible. The main tenets of IDEA include: identification and evaluation, zero rejection of students, personal development, technology-related assistance, free and appropriate public education, least restrictive environment, and, where necessary, placement in private schools.

Clarification of "Free and Appropriate Public Education"

A perplexing issue for parents and educators has been the phrase "free, appropriate education." To some extent this concept was clarified by the U.S. Supreme Court in *Board of Education of the Hendrick Hudson Central School District v. Rowley* (1982). In this case the parents of a student with minimal residual hearing had requested that the school district provide a sign-language interpreter for their daughter in her academic classes. The child's IEP specified a regular first-grade placement with special instruction from a tutor for the deaf one hour per day and a speech therapist three hours per week, but did not include interpreter services. An interpreter had been provided during a two-week period when the child was in kindergarten, but the service was discontinued based on recommendations of the interpreter and other teachers working with the child.

The Court held that "free appropriate public education" is satisfied when the state provides personalized instruction with *sufficient* support services to permit the disabled child to benefit educationally from that instruction. The instruction and services must be provided at public expense and in accord with the child's IEP. The significance of *Rowley* for school personnel is that the Court rejected the argument that school districts are required to provide the best possible education to disabled children.

Public Law 101-336: Americans with Disabilities Act

The last of the four significant laws approved by Congress was P.L. 101-336, the Americans with Disabilities Act (ADA). Approved in 1990, this legislation expanded into the private sector requirements for civil rights for students with disabilities.

Beginning with *Brown v. Board of Education* (1954), parents and advocacy groups have won many battles to obtain services for their children. Two key points were used in the argument for these services. The first, as noted earlier, was that many students with disabilities were receiving no education at all. The second was that there is a difference in the education needed by students with particular disabilities (Yell, 1998). These were powerful arguments in the struggle to win a free public education for all students. The requirement that schools develop an individualized education program (IEP) for each identified special education student established specific road maps for the education of disabled children.

California Master Plan for Special Education

In response to the federal legislation, each state was required to develop a master plan to provide for the education of children with special needs. The California legislature approved Senate Bill 1870 in 1980. This legislation was created to implement a statewide Master Plan for Special Education. The plan, begun as a pilot program in 1975-76, underwent several major changes between 1975-76 and 1979-80. It was implemented statewide in 1980.

The master plan was designed to provide flexibility in program and funding. The program side of the plan requires that, prior to placing a child in a special education program, a district must conduct an assessment to determine whether the child is most appropriately served in a special education setting or in the regular classroom. If special education services are needed, an individualized education program (IEP) is written for that pupil, describing the program to be provided. The IEP matches placement and services to a student's individual needs, instead of, as occurred all too often in the former system, placing him or her in a program based solely on the label for a particular handicapping condition.

The Individualized Education Program (IEP)

Requiring teachers to develop an Individualized Education Program for each student identified as having a disability was a major milestone in the education of special education students. All aspects of the special education program are directed and monitored by the IEP. If the IEP does not properly address the student's needs, then according to the courts, the student's special education program is not valid. The purposes of this plan include: communication, accountability, compliance, monitoring, and evaluation.

Although IEP format may differ slightly by district, certain components must be included in every IEP:

- goals and objectives that are annualized and include benchmarks
- specific services and service providers to be provided to the student
- present levels of educational performance, including instruments that determined this level
- dates that show the beginning and duration dates of services
- statements indicating how the student's progress is to be related to the parents
- how the least restrictive environment requirement is to be met.

An IEP assessment team should include the student's special education and regular education teachers, a representative of the school district, the parents, and, if appropriate, the student. Particular state mandates that work in concert with the IDEA must also be adhered to.

Related Services

Under IDEA, states must ensure that all children with disabilities receive a free and appropriate education. To this end, school districts are required to provide related services to identified disabled students as specified in the IEP. Such services may include speech pathology, audiology, psychological and physical assistance, and occupational therapy. Related services may also include therapeutic recreation, social work services, counseling, and medical services for diagnostic and evaluation purposes (Wenhart, 1989).

In *Irving Independent School District v. Tatro* (1984), the U.S. Supreme Court reviewed the meaning of related services. Amber Tatro was born with spina bifida. She suffered from orthopedic and speech impairments and a neurogenic bladder, which prevented her from emptying her bladder voluntarily. Therefore, catheterization was required every three or four hours to avoid injury to her kidneys.

The Supreme Court found that catheterization was essential in that it would enable the child to attend school and benefit from instruction. The Court held further that clean, intermittent catheterization was a related service, as it could be provided by a lay person and did not require the services of a physician. The Court noted that Congress did not intend that school districts be required to provide medical services that might be unduly expensive or beyond their range of competence. Nevertheless, school districts must provide education for children with serious medical needs, either in their home or in a hospital.

Finally, federal regulations require transportation of disabled students to and from school, even if specialized equipment is needed. A student qualifies for transportation if such service is provided for other similarly situated children or if included in the IEP. Failure to provide service to identified disabled students has resulted in courts requiring districts to reimburse parents their costs plus interest for transportation, time, effort, and babysitting.

Residential Placement

The IDEA and federal regulations require school districts to pay for residential placement in nonpublic facilities, if such placements are necessary for the disabled child to benefit from special education. The school district must pay the cost of the program, including non-medical care and room and board. However, where the primary reason for the child's placement is medical, not educational, the school district is not liable.

The case of *Capistrano Unified School District v. Wartenberg* (1995) illustrates the complexities of this issue. (Note that the school district is listed as plaintiff because the case is on appeal; the original plaintiffs were, of course, the student and his parents.) Jeremy was failing in school. The district increased special education services. When these did not help, the district concluded that the student's difficulties were a result of his misbehavior, not of his learning disability, and proposed reducing special education services. The parents disagreed and, without district concurrence, placed their son in a private school certified by California to serve special education students. They then sued the district for the costs of private school and for their attorney's fees. The U.S. District Court found for the parents and required the district to reimburse Jeremy's parents for costs of tuition and transportation.

The Ninth Circuit Court of Appeals outlined the legal issues: first, whether Jeremy's failure in school was the result of his learning disability or his misbehavior;

second, whether in relation to the learning disability the public school had provided an appropriate program; and third, whether the district court had used appropriate procedures in reaching its decision. The court affirmed the district court in its procedures, in its conclusion that Jeremy's difficulties resulted from his learning disability, and finally, in its finding that the proposed IEP did not allow sufficient time in special services to address Jeremy's needs. In taking this position, the court rejected an argument on the district's part citing the importance of mainstreaming. On the basis of an earlier Supreme Court decision, the appeals court awarded costs of schooling and attorney fees to the Wartenbergs.

Disciplining Students with Disabilities

A perplexing and important topic relative to education of disabled students is that of student discipline. This topic finds administrators and advocacy groups at odds. Special education laws do not exempt children from discipline for misbehavior unless that conduct is disability-related or the disciplinary punishment will defeat the purposes of those laws. Case law suggests that punishment is permissible for conduct that is within a child's reasonable control. However, the courts appear to favor less drastic action than the normal discipline procedures of suspension or expulsion for identified special education students.

Two provisions of the Education for All Handicapped Children Act must be considered when disciplinary action is taken with disabled students: free appropriate education and least restrictive environment. Acceptable environments for placement of a disabled student range from least restrictive (a regular classroom) to highly restrictive (an institution). Each environment may be termed least restrictive, depending on the seriousness of a particular handicap and on the child's ability to cope within the environment.

A 1997 amendment to IDEA finally addressed this issue. The amendment permits many disciplinary procedures for special education students, including detention, exclusionary time-outs, reprimands, and in-school suspension. However, except in isolated cases, long-term expulsions are not allowed unless it can be shown that the disability and the behavior are unrelated.

In *Honig v. Doe* (1988), the U.S. Supreme Court prohibited a school district from unilaterally excluding a disabled student from the classroom for an indeterminate period of time when dangerous or disruptive conduct is related to the student's disability. However, the Court did allow school districts to suspend a student for up to ten days to protect the safety of others and to provide a "cooling down period."

Graduation of Special Education Students

The courts have generally upheld state laws that require disabled students to pass a minimal competency test before they may receive a high school diploma. However, districts are required to give sufficient notice to the students of this requirement. In California, the Education Code gives districts the opportunity to establish differential standards for special education students. These standards must be included in the IEP. When a student achieves satisfactory progress on the differential standards, he or she may receive a certificate or document of educational achievement. A special education student who meets the criteria for a certificate may also participate in the graduation ceremony (Education Code 56390-56391).

Attorney Fees

The courts may award "reasonable" attorney fees to parents who prevail against a school district in a hearing or court action. The fees were permitted by a 1986 amendment entitled the Handicapped Children's Protection Act (HCPA). The amendment was approved because the Congress felt that without it, the cost of attorney fees could make parents reluctant to raise valid complaints challenging school district actions. Although this amendment has provided the resources for many parents to initiate a lawsuit, it has placed a financial drain on many school districts, since the parents' attorney fees can run into hundreds of thousands of dollars.

Continuing Lawsuits

As indicated in this chapter, parents of children with disabilities continue to turn to the courts in their attempt to force school districts to provide an educational program for their children. Although lawsuits against educational institutions nationwide have been declining, litigation involving special education continues to rise. A study by Lehigh's Zirkel (1999) found that special education lawsuits rose at a dramatic rate in the 1980s and a moderate rate in the 1990s. About a third of education litigation in federal courts in recent years has involved special education (Dolan, 1999). Parents of special education students bring lawyers to school meetings, and teachers have had to learn to work with the parent who brings a tape recorder to an IEP meeting.

In one case now on appeal, a school district in Santa Barbara County was ordered to pay the educational costs of a student in juvenile detention at a residential facility for troubled boys. The school had disciplined the boy for such offenses as possession of a razor knife, choking another student, and telling a teacher's aide to perform a sexual act with him. The attorney for the student said that the 14-year-old developed problems because the school district failed to provide him with appropriate services for a learning disability, and the court agreed. This case is presented as just one example of the ongoing conflict between parents who believe that a district is not providing their child with an appropriate educational program and district personnel who disagree with the perceived need or argue that the district does not have resources to meet the need.

Summary

This chapter has reviewed major laws and court cases that have provided a foundation for special education programs in effect today. Some of the most perplexing issues for the school administrator are those relating to the discipline of special education students. Since an IEP team has formulated the student's plan, this same team would best be involved in disciplinary procedures. The process is complex because the due process rights of these students must be observed, observational data must be written, and disciplinary actions applied in a nondiscriminatory manner.

Key Terms

1. ADA
2. California Master Plan
3. FAPE
4. HCPA
5. IDEA
6. IEP
7. inclusion
8. least restrictive environment
9. mainstreaming
10. P. L. 94-142
11. related services

Discussion / Essay Questions

1. Why was *Brown v. Board of Education* considered key to later special education law?

2. What issues with respect to educational placement of a child with disabilities might lead to contention between parents and school administrators?

3. Present three arguments to show why disciplining special education students can present a legal liability issue for the school administrator.

4. Why is the IEP so important for the education of special education students? What educational theories underlie its structure?

5. Do you believe that school districts should be required to pay the legal fees for parents when there is a dispute between the district and parents? Support your answer by citing appropriate statutes and case law.

References

Dolan, Maura. (1999, October 13). Disabled pupils get their day in court. *Los Angeles Times.*

McCarthy, M. M., Cambron-McCabe, N. H., & Thomas, S. B. (1998). *Public school law* (4th ed.). Needham Heights, MA: Allyn & Bacon.

Wenhart, R. D. (1989). *The California educators' guide to school law* (2nd ed.). Costa Mesa, CA: Orange County Department of Education.

Yell, M.L. (1998). *The law and special education.* Upper Saddle River, NJ: Merrill.

Zirkel, P. (1999). Fatal suspension. *Phi Delta Kappan, 80*, 791-792.

Court Cases

Armijo v. Wagon Mound Public Schools, 159 F.3d 1253 (10th Cir. 1998)

Board of Education of the Hendrick Hudson Central School District v. Rowley, 458 U.S. 176, 201,102 S.Ct. 3034, 3048 (1982)

Brown v. Board of Education of Topeka, 347 U.S. 483 (1954)

Capistrano Unified School District v. Wartenberg, 59 F.3d 884 (9th Cir. 1995)

Honig v. Doe, 484 U.S. 305, 108 S.Ct. 592 (1988)

Irving Independent School District v. Tatro, 468 U.S. 883, 104 S.Ct. 3371 (1984)

Mills v. Board of Education of the District of Columbia, 348 F. Supp. 866, 874 (D.D.C. 1972)

Pennsylvania Association for Retarded Citizens (PARC) v. Commonwealth of Pennsylvania, 343 F.Supp. 279 (E.D. Pa. 1972)

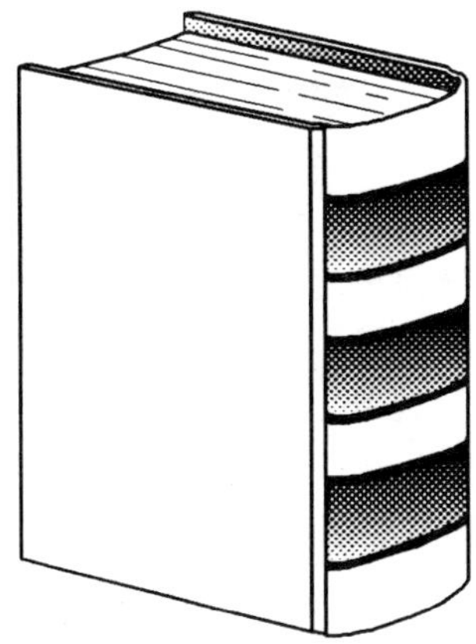

Chapter 7

Sexual Harassment in Education

Introduction

A high school auto shop teacher is accused by one of his students of asking her out for dates and refusing to take "no" for an answer. He is married, but within three months of the accusation his wife has filed for divorce, and he has been fired from his job. A school head custodian is accused of creating a hostile sexual atmosphere in the employee lounge by bringing to work some of his old *Playboy* magazines. The district fires him because of this incident. A student calls another student a "bitch" and is expelled from the district for his action. Are these examples of sexual harassment? Was the district within its legal rights when it dismissed the employee and expelled the student?

It is clear that sexual harassment is becoming a major concern to school districts. This chapter addresses the definition of sexual harassment, the historical evolution of its significance in the workplace, its various forms (student to student, staff member to staff member, school district employee to student), and court decisions that address the issue.

Definition of Sexual Harassment

Sexual harassment has not been clearly defined in legislation or by the courts. In 1986 the Supreme Court, in *Meritor Savings Bank v. Vinson*, defined sexual harassment as "a form of discrimination." The Court recognized for the first time that a violation of Title VII of the Civil Rights Act of 1964 can be predicated on "harassment that creates a hostile or offensive working environment in addition to harassment that involves receiving employment benefits based on granting sexual favors." The Court noted that conduct unreasonably interfering with an individual's work performance or creating an intimidating, hostile, or offensive working environment is actionable. Furthermore, the employer may not use as a defense the fact that the individual voluntarily engaged in sex-related conduct.

The Equal Employment Opportunity Commission (EEOC) provides guidelines to government entities, where sexual harassment is defined as "unwelcome sexual advances, requests for sexual favors, and/or other verbal or physical conduct of a sexual nature when . . ."—and here the EEOC uses the language set forth in subsection (a), section 1604.11, of the Civil Rights Act of 1964 (see Table 3).

There are two forms of sexual harassment: *quid pro quo* harassment and creation of a hostile sexual atmosphere. *Quid pro quo* literally means "something for something." In federal law, Title IX of the Education Amendments of 1972 prohibits unwelcome sexual behavior by any party who is in an inherently unequal position in relation to another. Because they are in a position to affect students' grades, academic attainments, and career choices, teachers hold power over students. Therefore, an example of *quid pro quo* harassment occurs if a teacher offers a student an A grade in return for sexual favors. The second category of harassment, "hostile sexual atmosphere," is more difficult to define, but occurs when a student or employee is mistreated solely due to gender.

Federal Laws Related to Sexual Harassment

The major federal statutes prohibiting sexual harassment include:

- The Equal Protection Clause of the Fourteenth Amendment to the Constitution
- Title VII of the Civil Rights Act of 1964
- Title IX of the Education Amendment of 1972.

The federal administrative agencies that handle complaints are the Equal Employment Opportunity Commission (EEOC) and the Office of Civil Rights (OCR).

The Fourteenth Amendment

Already quoted earlier in this book, the Fourteenth Amendment to the U.S. Constitution provides that

> No State shall make or enforce any law which shall abridge the privileges or immunities of citizens of the United States; nor shall any State deprive any person of life, liberty, or property, without due process of law; nor deny to any person within its jurisdiction the equal protection of the laws.

This provision, known as the "Equal Protection Clause," provides the basis for federal legislation and regulations governing state and local governmental agencies, including school districts, on issues such as opportunity for employment and equal access to public services.

Civil Rights Act of 1964

Since Title VII of the Civil Rights Act of 1964 (Section 1604.11) is the basis of sexual harassment suits, it is important to know the official text of the law, which is reproduced in Table 3. It will be noted that this legislation applies primarily to the working environment.

Title IX Regulations of 1972

Just as Title VII of the Civil Rights Act of 1964 prohibits sexual discrimination in the workplace, Title IX of 1972, a part of the Education Amendments, prohibits sexual discrimination in educational programs that are supported with federal monies. The law addresses harassment of an employee by an employee and harassment of a student by an employee or another student. Title IX is credited with sparking a revolution in women's sports. To achieve gender equity, high schools and colleges were forced to greatly expand and improve their athletic programs for women. More recently, women's rights lawyers have also looked to Title IX as a means of protecting students from sexual harassment. They have brought damage claims against school systems that failed to prevent sexual harassment of female students, whether by teachers or others.

Evolution in the Workplace

The Civil Rights Acts of 1964 and its 1988 amendments were important milestones in defining sexual harassment and making it illegal. Subsequent court decisions have profoundly affected the interpretation of the law (French, 1998).

The initial cases of sexual harassment emerged from private industry. The Equal Employment Opportunity Commission issued guidelines in 1980 clarifying the illegal aspects of sex-related behaviors. As noted earlier, the U.S. Supreme Court broadened the definition of sexual harassment in the case of *Meritor Savings Bank v. Vinson* (1986). In this case, the Court determined that sexual harassment occurs not only when employment or salary level is threatened, but also if an "intimidating, hostile, or offensive working environment" is created by sex-related behaviors.

Sexual harassment cases in private industry have become commonplace, especially in the last decade. An example is a suit against the law firm of Baker and McKensie of San Francisco in which the firm was ordered to pay $3.5 million for sexual harassment. Another example that received widespread media coverage was a lawsuit filed by a male employee at a hot tub manufacturing company in Los Angeles. His claim, for which he was awarded $1 million, was based on an allegation that the chief financial officer, a female, made regular sexual advances that the plaintiff found unwelcome and refused.

High profile cases have made Americans more aware of sexual harassment in the workplace. The topic again captured national attention when Justice Clarence Thomas, then a Supreme Court nominee, was accused of having sexually harassed a former employee and colleague, Anita Hill. Another event that triggered attention was the U.S. Navy's Tailhook scandal, involving sexual harassment of women attending a naval conference. In yet another case, a well-established restaurant declared bankruptcy when a waitress brought suit against a supervisor.

Such stories have rocked industry, especially in the past ten years, and have had a profound effect on the workplace. Consequently, there has been a major shift in the way supervisors think about sexual harassment (Maidment, 1998). Business managers and executives have increased their understanding of the seriousness of sexual harassment charges. Many employers have sought to reduce the chance that their business will be sued. These employers have developed a policy and made certain that all employees understand it. They have taken steps to inform employees that their jobs will not be adversely affected if they lodge a complaint.

Table 3.
Text of the Civil Rights Act of 1964, Title VII, Section 1604.11

(a) Harassment on the basis of sex is a violation of Sec. 703 of Title VII. Unwelcome sexual advances, requests for sexual favors, and other verbal or physical conduct of a sexual nature constitute sexual harassment when (1) submission to such conduct is made either explicitly or implicitly a term or condition of an individual's employment, (2) submission to or rejection of such conduct by an individual is used for employment decisions affecting such individual, or (3) such conduct has the purpose or effect of substantially interfering with an individual's work performance or creating an intimidating, hostile, or offensive working environment.
(b) In determining whether alleged conduct constitutes sexual harassment, the Commission will look at the record as a whole and at the totality of the circumstances, such as the nature of the sexual advances and the context in which the alleged incidents occurred. The determination of the legality of a particular action will be made from the facts, on a case by case basis.
(c) Applying general Title VII principles, an employer, employment agency, joint apprenticeship committee or labor organization (hereinafter collectively referred to as "employer") is responsible for its acts and those of its agents and supervisory employees with respect to sexual harassment regardless of whether the specific acts complained of were authorized or even forbidden by the employer and regardless of whether the employer should have known of their occurrence. The Commission will examine the circumstances of the particular employment relationship and job functions performed by the individual in determining whether individual acts in either a supervisory or agency capacity occurred.
(d) With respect to conduct between fellow employees, an employer is responsible for acts of sexual harassment in the workplace where the employer (its agents or supervisory employees) knows or should have known of the conduct, unless it can be shown that immediate and appropriate corrective action was taken.
(e) An employer may also be responsible for the acts of non-employees, with respect to sexual harassment of employees in the workplace, where the employer (its agents or supervisory employees) knows or should have known of the conduct and fails to take immediate and appropriate corrective action. In reviewing these cases, the Commission will consider the extent of the employer's control and any other legal responsibility, which the employer may have with respect to the conduct of such non-employees.
(f) Prevention is the best tool for the elimination of sexual harassment. An employer should take all steps necessary to prevent sexual harassment from occurring, such as affirmatively raising the subject, expressing strong disapproval, developing appropriate sanctions, informing employees of their right to raise and how to raise the issue of harassment under Title VII, and developing methods to sensitize all concerned. Other related practices: Where employment opportunities or benefits are granted because of an individual's submission to the employer's sexual advances or request for sexual favors, the employer may be liable for unlawful sex discrimination against other persons who were qualified but denied that employment opportunity or benefit.

Governmental entities were latecomers to recognizing their responsibilities when sexual harassment occurs. As awareness grew, federal, state, and municipal government officials began to develop sexual awareness seminars and to develop policies to deal with this issue. However, school districts were slow to see the need for policy development and employee awareness.

California Laws Delated to Sexual Harassment

Major California laws regarding sexual harassment are included in the following:

- California Fair Employment and Housing Act
- California Education Code
- California Civil Code, Section # 51.9 and following
- California Common Law Causes of Action

The administrative agency that handles many of these cases is the Department of Fair Employment and Housing.

Staff Member to Staff Member Sexual Harassment

Closest to the cases in private industry are instances of harassment from staff member to staff member in a school or district. Following is a situation that involved charges of sexual harassment at the highest level—between the superintendent and the chief financial officer.

According to the *Abilene Reporter-News*, the Dallas School Board had faced an unusual situation in 1997. The chief financial officer, Matthew Harden, Jr., alleged that the superintendent, Yvonne Gonzalez, had sexually harassed him and intentionally ruined the careers of several competent district employees. There were 154,985 students in the Dallas school system: 41.5 % black, 45.5% Hispanic, and slightly more than 10% White. In its decision to hire Gonzalez, the school board had split along racial lines; she had not received the support of the black community in her appointment.

In his suit against the district board, board president, and superintendent, Harden, who is black, alleged that Gonzalez made "personal overtures" to him and placed a tracking device on his car because "she was jealous of other women around him." Harden also claimed that Gonzalez sent him suggestive notes, such as "How about a little one-on-one?" The suit also alleged that although Gonzalez was already married, she wanted to marry Harden.

Gonzalez responded that Harden's lawsuit was an attempt to discredit her because of an ongoing probe into district corruption and mismanagement. At the time, Harden's division was the subject of internal and FBI investigations involving allegations of overtime abuse, contract fixing, and other problems. Several of Harden's top staffers had been placed on administrative leave or fired. All thirteen employees indicted on federal charges of overtime fraud were in Harden's division.

In the case of staff versus staff charges of sexual harassment, EEOC guidelines apply, as the issues involve "unwelcome sexual advances, requests for sexual favors, and other verbal and physical conduct." In this case Gonzalez was placed on administrative leave while the charges were investigated.

In February 1998, the suit was settled out of court. Harden received $600,000 in exchange for dropping his suits against the board and the board president and resigning. In the meantime, Superintendent Gonzalez had resigned and then pleaded guilty to a charge of using district funds to purchase personal furniture ("Dallas Independent," 1998).

Employee to Student Harassment

Perhaps the most serious cases of sexual harassment occur when a school employee sexually harasses a student. The fact that students are under the care of adults and the school district greatly contributes to the seriousness of such abuse. In addition to criminal charges filed against the employee, districts are being held liable in these cases.

Franklin v. Gwinnett County Public Schools

In 1998, in *Franklin v. Gwinnett County Public Schools*, the U.S. Supreme Court indicated that a student deserves as much protection from sexual harassment by a teacher as does an employee from harassment by a supervisor. The *Franklin* case alleged teacher-to-student harassment. Petitioner Christine Franklin was a student at North Gwinnett High School in Gwinnett County, Georgia, between 1985 and 1989. Christine charged that Andrew Hill, a sports coach and teacher, engaged her in sexually-oriented conversations and coerced her to submit to intercourse. She also charged that the school district was aware of Hill's actions, took no action to halt it, and discouraged Franklin from pressing charges against Hill. The Court ruled that monetary damages are an allowable award for a successful claim of sexual harassment.

Gebser et al. v. Lago Vista Independent School District

In June of 1998 an additional and significant question regarding district liability was decided by the Supreme Court in *Gebser et al. v. Lago Vista Independent School District*. This decision determined when a school district may be held liable for damages in an implied right of action under Title IX of the Education Amendments of 1972. The case involved sexual harassment of a student by a district teacher. The Court ruled that damages may not be recovered in those circumstances unless an official of the school district, who at a minimum has authority to institute corrective measures on the district's behalf, has had actual notice of, and is deliberately indifferent to, the teacher's misconduct.

The case involved a student who had a relationship with a teacher over a period of time. The petitioner, Alida Gebser, was an eighth-grade student at a middle school in Lago Vista Independent School District. The district received federal funds at the time, thus falling under the requirements of Title IX. Gebser joined a high school book discussion group led by Frank Waldrop, a teacher at Lago Vista's high school. During the book discussion sessions, Waldrop made sexually suggestive comments to the students. Gebser entered high school in the fall and was enrolled in classes taught by Waldrop in both of her freshman semesters.

The suit alleged that Waldrop continued making suggestive comments to Gebser and spent much time alone with her in the classroom. He initiated sexual contact with Gebser in the spring when, while visiting her home to give her a book, he kissed and fondled her. The two had sexual relationships on a number of occasions during the remainder of the school year. Their relationship lasted for several months and they often had intercourse during class time, although never on school property.

In January of 1993 charges were filed against Waldrop for engaging in sexual relations with Gebser. Lago Vista terminated his employment and, subsequently, the Texas Education Agency revoked his teaching license. The district during this time had not distributed a formal anti-harassment policy, nor did it have a procedure for lodging complaints. Gebser and her mother filed suit against the district and Waldrop in state court in November of 1993 citing Title IX and state negligence law. They sought compensatory and punitive damages from both defendants, primarily under state law.

Upon appeal to the U.S. Supreme Court, Justice Sandra Day O'Connor, who wrote the Court's opinion, stated, "No one questions that a student suffers extraordinary harm when subjected to sexual harassment and abuse by a teacher and the teacher's conduct is reprehensible." She continued, "Teachers who prey on students can be disciplined, fired, or even jailed in the worst cases, but the school system should not be required to pay large judgements for abuse of which it was unaware." The Court concluded its analysis by reaffirming that "school districts are not liable in tort for teacher-student sexual harassment under title IX unless an employee who has been invested by the school board with supervisory power over the offending employee actually knew of the abuse, had the power to end the abuse, and failed to do so."

The *Lago Vista* case further established that while compensatory damages are available in theory, they may be difficult to obtain in practice. The opinion suggested that in cases of teacher-student harassment, the school's liability may be restricted (Bussa, 1999).

Student-to-Student Harassment

Student-to-student harassment has created a challenge to school authorities. On February 14, 1996, Judge Barkett, writing for the Eleventh Circuit, held that the Monroe County Board of Education was in violation of Title IX, having allowed a "hostile environment" form of sexual harassment. This case was the first Court of Appeals decision to allow the possibility of damages for student-to-student harassment. However, the decision was further modified by other court decisions, as we shall see shortly.

Davis v. Monroe County Board of Education

The Eleventh Circuit Court, in the case of *Davis v. Monroe County Board of Education* (1999), extended the established rule in *Franklin* to include the "hostile environment" protection of Title VII as compensable under Title IX. LaShonda, a fifth-grade female, had been sexually harassed by a fellow fifth-grade boy, G.F., for a period of six months between December 1992 and May 1993. Over this period, G.F. fondled LaShonda and directed sexually offensive language toward her. In December, for example, G.F. attempted to touch LaShonda's breasts and vaginal area, telling her "I want to get in bed with you" and "I want to feel your boobs." Two similar incidents occurred in January 1993. In February, G.F. placed a doorstop in his pants and behaved in a sexually suggestive manner toward LaShonda. Other incidents occurred later in February and in March. In April, G.F. rubbed up against LaShonda in the hallway in a sexually suggestive manner. G.F.'s actions increased in severity until he finally was charged with and pled guilty to sexual battery in May 1993.

LaShonda and her mother reported the incidents to both the teacher and the school principal. Other female students reported that G.F. had sexually harassed them. Neither the principal nor the teacher took remedial action to assist LaShonda or to correct G.F. Even LaShonda's request to move her seat so as not to be next to G.F. was refused for three months. He was never removed or disciplined in any way by school authorities.

The claim for damages was based upon allegations that G.F.'s uncurbed and unrestrained conduct severely curtailed LaShonda's ability to benefit from her elementary school education, lessening her capacity to concentrate on her schoolwork and causing her grades, previously all A's and B's, to deteriorate. The harassment had a debilitating effect on her mental and emotional well-being, leading her to write a suicide note in April of 1993.

The court found liability because the board had no policy and the teacher and principal took no action. The *Davis* court noted that a "female student should not be required to run a gauntlet of sexual abuse in return for being allowed to obtain an education." The court combined the Title VII doctrine regarding a sexually hostile working environment created by coworkers and tolerated by the employer with the Title IX requirements for protection of students.

Previous rulings by the federal court system had supported a broad application of Title VII guidelines for this purpose. In reaching their conclusions, some courts had interpreted the "intentional conduct" requirement (traditionally necessary for institutional liability) to read "callous indifference" in the case of educational institutions. Thus, indifference has come to meet the "intentional" requirement when school officials do not respond to complaints and fail to take prompt action to stop harassment.

In the *Davis* case, the court reasoned that when an educational institution knowingly fails to take action to remedy a hostile environment caused by a student's sexual harassment of another, the harassed student has "been denied the benefits of, or been subjected to discrimination under" that educational program. This extension of the *Franklin* doctrine created a significant media response. For example, primarily as a result of this decision, an article in the August 1996 *Reader's Digest* by Daniel Levine named Judge Barkett one of seven of America's worst judges. Levine quotes Clint Bolick, litigation director of the Institute for Justice in Washington DC, as follows:

> Decisions like this could cost taxpayers untold millions. Unless the decision is overturned or Congress amends the statute, every school district in America is at risk of schoolyard bullies exposing them to federal lawsuits.

The complexity of these issues may be noted, however, in that, subsequent to its 1996 decision, the Eleventh Circuit Court agreed to rehear the matter and reversed itself, thus dismissing the case. Plaintiffs appealed to the U.S. Supreme Court, which in May 1999 determined that private action for damages may be pursued against a school board, but "only for harassment that is so severe, pervasive, and objectively offensive that it effectively bars the victim's access to an educational opportunity" and, in addition, the federally-funded district acts with "deliberate indifference to known acts of harassment." The case was then remanded to the Circuit Court, which in March of 2000 sent it back to the original court for trial.

Petaluma v. Jane Doe

A highly publicized case of student-to-student harassment was that of *Petaluma v. Jane Doe* (1993). Jane Doe was a junior high school student in the Petaluma City School District in Sonoma County, California. Throughout seventh and eighth grade, other students allegedly harassed her sexually.

In fall of 1990, during her seventh-grade year, two boys said to her, "I hear you have a hot dog in your pants." Another student informed her that a rumor was spreading around the school about her "having a hot dog in her pants." Jane Doe reported this information to her guidance counselor, saying that she was very upset. He did nothing. She was continually harassed thereafter and informed the guidance counselor of this every other week. He stated that all he could do was warn the boys. He did not tell her that the vice-principal was the school's Title IX coordinator and was the appropriate person to handle the situation, nor did he tell her of the Title IX grievance procedure.

Toward the end of the semester, Jane's mother and father spoke to the counselor about the rumors. The parents described the behavior of several students who were calling Jane names, writing graffiti about her in the restrooms, and otherwise constantly harassing their daughter. The counselor replied that he was taking care of the problem. However, the harassment continued for several months, until the district's Title IX coordinator finally heard the case.

Eventually, Jane was transferred to another junior high school. She continued to be the subject of harassment. At this point, Jane's parents felt they had no choice but to enroll her in a private school. They filed suit in federal court to be compensated by the school district for monetary damages, including Jane's private school tuition and the costs of medical and psychological treatment.

The basis of their suit was Title IX of the Educational Amendments of 1972, which prohibits sexual discrimination by school districts and other entities that receive federal funds. For this purpose they relied to a significant extent on *Franklin v. Gwinnett County Public Schools* (1992). In addition, they claimed that the school district, principal, and counselor had violated Jane's substantive due process rights under the Fourteenth Amendment. According to the National Organization of Women (NOW), the case was settled out of court in January 1997 for $250,000 ("Landmark," 1997). Although the case did not go to trial, NOW hailed it as "the first to affirm that schools are responsible for responding to sexual harassment by students." On the other hand, it should be noted that on appeal to the Northern District of California, a requirement was established that a district must have known or should have known of the harassment in order to be held liable.

Certainly the more recent Supreme Court statement regarding *Davis v. Monroe County Board of Education* (1999), discussed above, underscores that responsibility, while at the same time setting stringent requirements for interference with the harassed student's educational opportunities. Regardless of variations in interpretation of these conditions, recent cases have consistently emphasized that students may not be excluded from participation, denied benefits, or discriminated against because of sex.

Appropriate School Board Actions

It is the responsibility of all school board members, school officials, teachers, and school employees to maintain an environment that is free of sexual harassment. A number of steps can be taken to ensure a work environment that is free of sexual harassment and, should such behavior occur, an appropriate response. The first requirement is adoption of a sexual harassment policy that includes a definition of sexual harassment and the proper procedures to follow should it occur. The second requirement is designation of officials charged with the responsibility for immediately investigating and taking appropriate action to remedy any reported sexual harassment. A third requirement is that the district provide an ongoing series of information meetings for staff regarding sexual harassment and the proper procedures to be followed if and when investigation or action becomes necessary.

SUMMARY

Sexual harassment has become a very important aspect of American society. Over the past few decades this issue has received generous media attention. As a consequence, awareness of the serious nature of sexual harassment has greatly increased. Employers and employees have become aware that unwanted touching, unwanted comments, and even the display of *Playboy* magazine are unacceptable conduct in many settings, including educational institutions.

Sexual harassment can take many forms: student-to-student, employee-to-employee, and employee-to-student. All districts must take positive, proactive steps to ensure that all students and employees are provided with an environment free of sexual harassment. Proactive steps include policies, procedures, and information programs to deal with the issue. School districts have joined other government agencies and private industry in informing employees of conduct that may be sexual harassment. Supervisors have also been informed of procedures to follow when they become aware of behavior that may be a form of sexual harassment.

The Office of Civil Rights (OCR) is the federal agency that ensures that schools comply with Title IX. Students who believe they are being sexually harassed and feel the school district is not taking appropriate action should contact one of the OCR offices to receive information about filing a complaint. School administrators should also contact one of these offices for technical assistance. This agency has posted a list of some frequently asked questions about sexual harassment, available on the Internet at http://www.ed.gov/offices/OCR/faqs.html.

Key Terms

1. Equal Employment Opportunity Commission
2. hostile sexual atmosphere
3. Office of Civil Rights
4. *quid pro quo* sexual harassment
5. Title VII of the Civil Rights Act of 1964
6. Title IX of the Education Amendments of 1972

Discussion / Essay Questions

1. What are the grievance procedures that a student in your district should follow when sexually harassed by another student?

2. A recent Supreme Court decision has clarified the issue of school district liability in sexual harassment cases. What is this Supreme Court case? How does the decision impact school district liability?

3. What is the difference between "*quid pro quo*" sexual harassment and "establishing a hostile environment" sexual harassment?

4. What is the United States Office of Civil Rights? How does this office relate to sexual harassment claims?

References

Busa, A. (1999). "Two steps forward, one step back: The Supreme Court's treatment of teacher-student sexual harassment in *Gebser v. Lago Vista Independent School District. Harvard Civil Rights–Civil Liberties Law Review, 34*, 279-309.

Dallas Independent School District board reaches settlement with chief financial officer. (1998, February 8). *Abilene Reporter-News.* Retrieved August 28, 2000, from the World Wide Web: http://www.reporternews.com/texas/disd0208.htm

French, W. L. (1998). *Human resources management.* Boston: Houghton Mifflin .

Landmark peer sexual harassment case settled on eve of trial. (1997, January 6). National Organization of Women. Retrieved August 28, 2000, from the World Wide Web http://www.nowldef.org/html/news/pr/010697e.htm

Maidment, F. H. (1998). *Human Resources, 1997-98.* Guilford, CT: McGraw Hill.

Court Cases

Davis v. Monroe County Board of Education, 74 F. 3d. 1186 (11th Cir. 1996), 120 F.3d 1390 (11th Cir. 1997), 119 S.Ct. 1661 (1999)

Franklin v. Gwinnett County Public Schools, 503 U.S. 60, 112 S.Ct. 1028 (1992)

Gebser et. al. v. Lago Vista Independent School District, 106 F.3rd 1223 (1998)

Meritor Savings Bank v. Vinson, 477 U.S. 57, 106 S.Ct. 2399 (1986)

Petaluma v. Jane Doe , 830 F. Supp. 1560 (N.D. Cal. 1993); U.S. Dist. (1993); Doe v. Petaluma City Sch. Dist., 1996 WL 432298 (N.D. Cal. July 22, 1996)

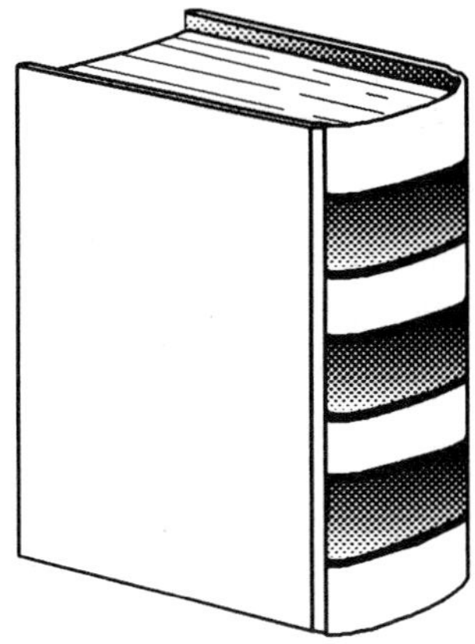

Chapter 8

Progressive Discipline and Dismissal of Employees

Introduction

To recruit, select, supervise, and retain highly effective certificated and classified employees is of primary importance to all school districts. However, even when these responsibilities are performed in an outstanding fashion, there comes a time in every school and every district when an employee is not performing in an acceptable manner. At that time a second mandate of every superintendent, district supervisor, and school principal falls into place. An administrator's first responsibility is to students—and the second, to staff. The second responsibility must not be allowed to override the first one.

Corrective action may take the form of employee discipline or dismissal from employment. This chapter begins with a brief description of employee supervision and evaluation. It then defines employee discipline and includes a discussion of the several categories of employment. The historical development of tenure is included, along with the arguments pro and con. The tasks of progressive discipline, non-renewal, and dismissal are discussed.

Employee Supervision and Evaluation

Education Code section 44664 requires evaluation and assessment of the performance of each certificated employee at least once each school year for probationary personnel, and least every other year for tenured personnel. If areas of improvement are identified, the evaluation must include recommendations for improvement. The evaluator must be very specific in describing expectations to be met.

As one can determine from the relevant Education Code sections, evaluation has two main purposes: (a) to determine the strengths and weaknesses of the employee so that strengths can be noted and deficiencies remedied, and (b) to document in one place data with which to make management decisions regarding teacher promotion, dismissal, non-renewal, transfer, demotion, withholding of salary increments, and tenure or continuing contract. The first of these is called "formative" evaluation; the second, "summative."

Formative evaluation is a first step in improving instruction. This task is the primary function of a school principal. The objective is to help each individual teacher develop to the optimum by strengthening existing skills while discovering and correcting weaknesses. Formative evaluation is the appraisal function principals use to develop or improve teaching performance.

Summative evaluation involves many of the techniques used in formative evaluation, but it goes further. For the competent teacher, it can be a positive recognition of commitment and growth. It seeks to build evidence on which educational decisions can be made; these may include change of assignment, professional growth opportunities, or leadership options. When a teacher seems to be doing less well, summative evaluation may require corrective action.

Although this chapter focuses on teachers, it should also be noted that principles such as formative and summative evaluation and processes such as progressive discipline apply as well to other certificated personnel and to classified staff. The procedures and timelines may vary, but the overall approach is the same.

Employee Discipline

The term "discipline" often carries a negative connotation. This negative aspect is found in the second part of Webster's definition: “punishment inflicted by way of correction and training; instruction by means of misfortune, suffering, and the like; correction; chastisement.” The first part of the dictionary definition is the positive part: “training, education, instruction, and the government of conduct or practice; the training to act in accordance with rules; drill; method of regulating principles and practice.”

School district employee discipline begins with the positive view. It is based on the premise and expectation that employees will conduct themselves according to the rules and regulations of the organization and in a socially accepted manner. When this does not occur, what is the appropriate supervisory response?

It is commonly accepted in business and industry that the response of management to unsatisfactory employee performance must be corrective, rather than punitive. It is also accepted that the action must be progressive if it is to withstand the test of due process under the Fourteenth Amendment. For example, if a teacher releases students from class early, the principal should give that teacher a verbal warning. If the teacher repeats the early dismissal the following week, the principal gives a written reprimand. If the teacher's behavior continues for the third week, the teacher might be suspended from work for a few days without pay. If the inappropriate behavior continues after the suspension period, the principal must continue with progressive discipline and finally recommend dismissal of the employee from the district.

The right of a school board to terminate an employee from service is clearly established in state statutes and confirmed by the courts. The U.S. Supreme Court bestowed this authority on school boards when it held that "school authorities have the right and the duty to screen the officials, teachers, and employees as to their fitness to maintain the integrity of the schools as part of ordered society" (*Adler v. Board of Education*, 1952). However, even with its authority to terminate employment, a board cannot arbitrarily discharge personnel at any time. Except in the case of an employee convicted of a criminal act or flagrant violation of board policy (in which cases action may be immediate), a district is required to document unsatisfactory performance, demonstrate efforts to improve performance, and follow a course of progressive discipline.

Progressive Discipline

When an employee is not performing in a satisfactory fashion, the central question is: What action, or series of actions, is appropriate to bring about adequate performance? There is a plethora of books and articles on changing inappropriate behavior through rewards, behavior modification, and staff development programs designed for the purpose. It is the judgment of the authors that those leadership techniques work with the great majority of employees. However, a supervisor must be prepared to take disciplinary action, including a recommendation for employee dismissal, when attempts to change behavior do not work.

Appropriate leadership and humane treatment of personnel call for corrective action when unsatisfactory performance occurs. Supervisors have a duty to provide training, informal correction and, if needed, formal discipline when rules or duties are not performed properly.

For example, if the district requires teachers to be on campus 30 minutes prior to the start of class, and a teacher is late one time in a semester, his tardiness probably would not even receive a rebuke for violation of the employee contract. However, positive, fair, and objective measures are required when a teacher is late on a regular basis and does not respond to a verbal reminder of the importance of being in class on time. Ruud and Woodford (1992) define progressive discipline as a general pattern of escalating disciplinary penalties designed to persuade or motivate an employee to improve performance or change behavior.

Andelson (1995) defines progressive discipline as "a series of disciplinary steps, each step calling for more serious disciplinary action." He proposes the following six levels of action.

1. Oral warning/ conference	The supervisor states clearly the rule or policy that has been violated, the expectation that the rule be followed, and the consequence if the rule is not followed in the future. The time, date, and substance of the warning are noted on a daily calendar or some other informal written record (not the employee's personnel file). An oral warning should be brief, to the point, and directly related to a specific incident.
2. Written warning	The written warning is similar to the oral warning and, if possible, delivered personally to the employee. One of the consequences of further violation of the rule or policy may be notice to the employee that an additional violation will result in a letter of reprimand to be placed in the employee's personnel file.
3. Letter of reprimand	The first two steps in the progressive discipline model generally do not result in placing information in the personnel file. However, a letter of reprimand is ordinarily placed there. The letter contains statements similar to those in the oral and written notice. In addition, the employee must be notified that the letter will be placed in the personnel file. He or she must have opportunity to review and respond to any document containing derogatory information. If the employee responds, that document is also placed in the personnel file (E.C. 44031). Although the law does not spell out a time limit for an employee's response to a letter of reprimand, the time is often regulated by the collective bargaining agreement—typically five to ten calendar days.

4. Unsatis-factory evaluation	The requirements for evaluation are outlined in the Education Code. Procedures are generally included in the collective bargaining agreement between the district and the employee association.
5. Suspension with pay	Suspension with pay is often a nondisciplinary step that provides time for an investigation to determine whether discipline is justified. Suspension with pay may also accompany a second reprimand to emphasize the seriousness of the infraction. Suspension without pay is practical for classified employees, but more difficult to administer with credentialed employees. The reason for this difficulty is that credentialed employees work under a contact, which creates a property right. As we have seen, the Fourteenth Amendment states that one cannot be deprived of property without due process.
6. Dismissal	A later section of this chapter is devoted to additional discussion of dismissal.

In summary, progressive discipline is a system of documentation and file-building that is divided into stages, each successive stage resulting in more serious disciplinary measures. Obviously, it is the responsibility of the supervisor to work extensively with an employee prior to recommending dismissal from service.

Probationary Status

District requirements for teacher dismissal differ, depending on the employee's classification as probationary or tenured. A teacher is considered to have probationary status prior to achieving tenure. During the probationary period, a teacher is issued a contract valid for a fixed period of time. California teachers are classed as "probationary" during the first two years of service within a school district (E.C. 44929.21). During this probationary period, renewal of the contract at the end of each school year is at the discretion of the school board.

Commonly, a probationary teacher is not entitled to know the reasons for which a school board has decided to terminate the employment relationship at the end of the contract period. In most cases, a probationary teacher is not given the opportunity for a hearing. Even though the school board is not compelled to inform the probationary teacher of the reasons for non-renewal, it is important to recognize that those reasons cannot violate the teacher's Constitutionally or statutorily protected rights.

The school board is required to notify a probationary employee on or before March 15th of the employee's second complete consecutive school year of employment of the decision not to reelect him or her for the next school year. If the board does not give notice on or before March 15th, the employee is deemed reelected for the next succeeding school year (E.C. 44929.21).

Tenure Status

Tenure is defined as a statutory right to continued employment. The employer must have proof of "good cause" prior to dismissal. As defined by *Black's Law Dictionary* (1999), tenure is "a status afforded to a teacher or professor as a protection against summary dismissal without sufficient cause." The 1992 *Deskbook Encyclopedia of American School Law* described tenure as a "creation of state statute designed to maintain adequate, permanent, and qualified teaching staffs."

Generally, tenure granted by the state means at least two things for a teacher: (a) continuing employment without the necessity of annual notification; and (b) if employment is to be terminated, adequate reasons for termination and an opportunity for an impartial hearing ensuring fundamental fairness. The decision of whether to recognize "tenure status" is left to the discretion of each state legislature.

Purpose of Tenure

Tenure provides security for a teacher. The academic rationale for tenure is that it gives the teacher academic freedom in the classroom. In addition, tenured teachers cannot be fired for holding and expressing, outside the classroom, unpopular political or social views. Tenure gives a teacher legal protection against unwarranted dismissal. An additional purpose served by tenure is to provide equity based on seniority when staff must be reduced because of lack of enrollment or finances; length of service is the criterion for dismissal.

History of Tenure

The concept of rewarding one's friends with jobs or positions of influence is part of early American history. During this country's Colonial period, the English government retained power by distributing jobs and influence to friends and supporters. This system of handing out jobs became known as the "spoils system" or "patronage."

The country's first President, George Washington, often made support of Federalist principles a test of appointment to office. When Jefferson became President, he complained of the number of Federalists he found holding jobs in the executive department and gradually replaced Federalists with Republicans. It was not until the presidency of Andrew Jackson that wholesale removal of jobholders was accomplished so that he could appoint his followers to office. This practice continued with each President; during the Civil War, President Lincoln expressed his frustration with the countless number of job seekers who filled his appointment schedule.

The system of awarding positions greatly accelerated after the Civil War and became a topic of national concern when President Garfield was assassinated by a half-crazy office seeker. This tragic event so excited the nation against the spoils system that in 1883 the Pendleton Act was passed by Congress. This law allowed the President to place on a "classified list" certain federal offices that then could be filled only according to rules laid down by a bipartisan Civil Service Commission. The Pendleton Act began the process of changing government employment from the spoils system to a merit system (Bragdon & McCutchen, 1961).

Gradually, the concept of employees gaining and retaining their jobs on merit spread to the states and local governments. It was out of this movement that the concept of tenure for teachers developed. In 1887 the proceeding of the National Education Association "carried a committee report urging that the subject of teachers' tenure be given publicity in the belief that necessary legislation would result" (National Education Association, 1936).

Thus, tenure had its beginning in the late 1880s. Tenure statutes protect teachers from arbitrary actions by local boards of education. In some states and school districts, other certificated personnel also are protected by tenure statutes. The selection of positions to be covered under tenure laws is within the prerogative of the state legislature. Employee classifications that may gain tenure rights include school nurses, counselors, psychologists, and school librarians. In some states, selected administrative positions may also obtain tenure. However, tenure is rarely granted to superintendents or assistant superintendents.

The courts have sustained the constitutionality of such statutes. Certificated Tenure Act cases have concluded that tenure exists to protect competent teachers and other members of the teaching profession against unlawful and arbitrary board actions and to provide orderly procedures for the dismissal of unsatisfactory teachers and other professional personnel (*Teachers Tenure Act Cases*, 1938).

Tenure is attained by complying with specific provisions prescribed by state statutes. The nature of these provisions varies from state to state, but certain conditions are included in most legislation. Nearly all states require that teachers serve a probationary period before tenure becomes effective. Generally, the probationary period ranges from three to five years, during which time a teacher is employed on a term contract. On completion of the probationary period, personnel acquire tenure, either automatically or by school board action.

Arguments For and Against Tenure

Tenure continues to be a matter of debate in the United States. Advocates strongly believe tenure is positive for children and teachers, while opponents believe it is detrimental to students and teachers. Jones and Stout (1960) advanced the following arguments in favor of and opposed to tenure.

Favorable arguments:

1. Tenure is a basic principle of economic efficiency.
2. Tenure helps to protect the teacher from unwarranted attacks.
3. The teacher is freed from anxiety over being dismissed without just cause.
4. Tenure helps parents and citizens to secure better teachers because it encourages a more careful selection of faculty.
5. There is little evidence that tenure reduces interest in professional development.
6. Tenure reduces the temptation for teachers to violate professional ethics and to yield to the whims of pressure groups.

Opposing arguments:

1. Incompetent and undesirable teachers may be retained in the profession, since tenure makes it more difficult to dismiss them.
2. It may become more difficult to supervise some teachers who know they have security of position.
3. Contrary to popular opinion, tenure has, in a number of instances, increased teacher turnover.
4. Tenure of office is not protected by law in other professions.
5. The public has, in many instances, questioned the practice of permitting teachers to hold their positions despite their failure to do a competent job.
6. Competent teachers do not need to be protected by tenure legislation.

Reduction in Force (RIF)

School districts are often faced with a variety of factors that require them to reduce staff. Declining enrollment is one example of a situation in which a district may need to layoff teachers or classified employees. The reduction may be temporary or permanent.

This practice is commonly referred to as "reduction in force" (RIF). The conditions in which a district may use RIF are contained in E.C. 44955. A district desiring to use this procedure has the burden of documenting the need to reduce staff in response to one or more of the legislated reasons, that is, declining enrollment, fiscal exigency, school district reorganization, or "other good and just cause."

Once the district has justified the RIF, the next step is determination of the order in which to release staff. For the most part, probationary employees are released prior to the dismissal of tenured employees. Seniority, defined as years of service in the school district or within a particular classification, is most frequently used to determine the order of lay-off of employees.

Non-Renewal and Dismissal

In discussing termination of employment of teachers and other certificated personnel, the terms "non-renewal" and "dismissal" are often used interchangeably. However, non-renewal is more properly applied to probationary teachers, while dismissal generally refers to termination of employment at any time.

There is a substantial difference in the manner of termination in each case. Courts have reasoned in non-renewal cases that the contract has simply terminated and there is no "expectancy of continued employment." Non-renewal usually requires that a school board simply give a probationary employee timely notice that his or her contract is not being renewed. In most states, the school board need not give reasons for the non-renewal of a probationary teacher (Hartmeister, 1995). If not protected by tenure, a school employee's contract may be non-renewed for any reason whatsoever or for no reason, providing the action does not violate an employee's substantive Constitutional rights, for example, right of free speech or to protection from racial discrimination.

Dismissal, on the other hand, whether under tenure status or during an unexpired contract, is permissible only "for cause." Because an employee has a Constitutionally protected property interest in remaining employed throughout the contract term, he or she is entitled to notification of reasons for the dismissal and an opportunity for a hearing in which to respond to or rebut all stated reasons.

Consequently, dismissal of a tenured employee or a non-tenured professional during a contract year calls for a fair and impartial due process hearing with all statutory and Constitutional safeguards.

Grounds for Dismissal

The most common grounds for the dismissal of teachers are incompetency, immorality, insubordination, unfitness to teach, and inadequate performance of duties. Conviction of a felony or a crime involving moral turpitude, or any cause that leads the state to revoke a teaching certificate, is also grounds for dismissal. Other grounds for dismissal include reduction in force, when a teacher's services are no longer needed due to declining enrollment or financial exigency. In addition, there is normally an "elastic" clause added to this list: "other good and just cause."

Causes for dismissal are generally specified in state statutes and differ from one state to another. However, there are similarities. For example, in Kentucky tenured employees can be dismissed for insubordination; immoral character or conduct; physical or mental disability; or inefficiency, incompetency, or neglect of duty. In Illinois, cause for dismissal is specified as incompetency, cruelty, negligence, immorality or other sufficient cause and whenever in the board's opinion a teacher is not qualified to teach or the best interests of the school require it. In Connecticut, causes enumerated are inefficiency, incompetency, insubordination, moral misconduct, disability as shown by competent medical evidence, elimination of positions, or for other due and sufficient cause. The school district has the burden of proving any charges and, to do so, must show persuasive evidence that the teacher being recommended for dismissal either failed to do something that he or should have done—or did something that he or should not have done.

Grounds for Dismissal of Certificated Employees in California

Education Code sections 44932 and 44933 are very specific regarding the grounds for dismissal of certificated employees. Twelve specific reasons are stated.

1. Immoral or unprofessional conduct

   Immoral conduct must be judged within the context of local standards, but also must be reasonable and consistent with court decisions. One of the standards used by the courts is the health of the pupil-teacher relationship. A teacher or other employee who establishes a relationship with a student that goes beyond friendship and is exhibited in some form of "dating" is unacceptable. Of course, illegal sexual acts are cause for immediate suspension. If an employee is convicted of performing such an act, his or employment must be terminated.

Nonconventional sexual life styles, however, are not a cause for employee dismissal. Such practices as wife swapping, homosexuality, and cohabitation outside of matrimony may be unacceptable to the majority of people in the community, but do not inherently affect an individual's performance in the workplace. However, if an employee advocates nonconventional sexual lifestyles at work, and those life styles are in direct conflict with local standards, he or she has placed himself or herself in a position such that termination is possible.

2. Commission, aiding, or advocating the commission of acts of criminal syndicalism

3. Dishonesty

4. Unsatisfactory performance

   A significant change was made in the grounds for dismissal in 1995. Assembly Bill 729 was approved by the legislature and signed by the Governor on August 10, 1995. The significant change was substituting "unsatisfactory performance" for "incompetency."

5. Evident unfitness for service

6. Physical or mental condition unfitting him or her to instruct or associate with children

7. Persistent violation of or refusal to obey the school laws of the state or reasonable regulations prescribed for the government of the public schools by the state Board of Education or by the governing board of the school district employing him or her

   Employees are insubordinate only if they refuse to comply with a directive of their supervisor that is clearly within their job expertise. Thus, if a teacher is directed to attend a faculty meeting and refuses, the teacher is insubordinate because teachers have a job-related responsibility in this area. However, if the teacher refuses to go to the principal's house to help with administrative paperwork, the teacher is not guilty of insubordination, as this task is not within the teacher's job assignment.

The manner in which the employee responds to a directive does not usually constitute insubordination if the employee performs the task. For example, if the teacher complains about grading papers, but completes the task, the teacher is not guilty of insubordination.

8. Conviction of a felony or of any crime involving moral turpitude

Conviction of a felony is a reason to terminate employment of an individual. In most states, a school district employee who is found guilty of a felony is considered in breach of his or her employment contract and can be dismissed from employment. The basis in breach of contract takes as its premise that teachers are expected to be positive role models for their students. Felony convictions are not congruent with this expectation and are obviously deleterious to a teacher's effectiveness. Courts have held on numerous occasions that a civil sanction, that is, loss of employment following a criminal conviction, does not violate the principle of double jeopardy set forth in the Fifth Amendment to the Constitution.

Courts have placed restrictions on the interpretation of moral turpitude. Nevertheless, conviction of prostitution, selling of drugs, or pornography do fall within the definition of moral turpitude (Rebore, 1998). District action is not as clearly defined when teachers are convicted of a misdemeanor, a crime less serious than a felony. Generally, an employee who has been arrested, but not convicted of a criminal offense, cannot be dismissed unless found guilty.

9. Advocacy of or inculcation into communism

E.C. 51530 reads as follows: "No teacher giving instruction in any school, or on any property belonging to any agencies included in the public school system, shall advocate or teach communism with the intent to indoctrinate or to inculcate in the mind of any pupil a preference for communism." The code section has a second paragraph stating that the legislature did not intend to prevent the teaching of the facts about communism, but to prevent the advocacy of, or inculcation and indoctrination into, communism. The third paragraph in this section defines communism: "Communism is a political theory that the presently existing form of government of the United States or of this state should be changed, by force, violence, or other unconstitutional means, to a totalitarian dictatorship which is based on the principles of communism expounded by Marx, Lenin, and Stalin."

10. Knowing membership by the employee in the Communist Party

11. Alcoholism or other drug abuse that makes the employee unfit to instruct or associate with children

12. Unprofessional conduct

    Unprofessional conduct is made grounds for suspension without pay in section 44932(b) and for dismissal in 44933. The latter includes the statement: "A permanent employee may be dismissed or suspended on grounds of unprofessional conduct consisting of acts or omissions other than those specified in Section 44932, but any such charge shall specify instances of behavior deemed to constitute unprofessional conduct."

Dismissal Procedures

If a school superintendent recommends dismissal of a tenured employee, the requirements of the Education Code must be followed precisely. The procedures are detailed and specific. They contain three basic elements: (a) notice of intention to dismiss by a specific date, (b) specification of charges against the employee (E.C. 44934), and (c) a hearing at which the charges are discussed (E.C. 44944).

The procedures for notifying the employee of the hearing and the hearing process are more detailed than can be included in this text. Prior to recommending dismissal of a tenured employee, the personnel director and superintendent should seek counsel from a county counsel or an attorney who specializes in school law.

Besides the procedures required in the Education Code, tenure rights qualify for Constitutional procedural protections encompassed within the concepts of property and liberty interests under the Due Process Clause of the Fourteenth Amendment. To hold a teaching position qualifies as a property right if the employee has an unexpired contract or has acquired tenure. The protections of the Fourteenth Amendment do not normally extend to non-tenured employees. The Supreme Court has affirmed the view of the courts that non-tenured employees have no property or liberty interests in continued employment (*Roth v. Board of Regents*, 1972).

A liberty interest would be an issue in dismissal, and due process is required when a charge has been made that might place a stigma on an employee's reputation, thus foreclosing future employment opportunities or seriously damaging the individual's standing in the community (*Roth v. Board of Regents*). A liberty interest is not at issue if school board members and school administrators refrain from making public statements or releasing information derogatory to the employee. Even when statements are made, if they simply mention unsatisfactory performance in general, they do not normally violate the employee's Fourteenth Amendment rights. Examples of charges against employees not involving stigma include ineffective teaching methods, inability to maintain classroom discipline, and inability to get along with administrators and colleagues. Failure to award tenure does not automatically create a stigma. Examples of stigmas that *do* qualify for Constitutional due process protection include the following charges: manifest racism, immoral conduct, serious mental disorder, a drinking or drug problem, willful neglect of duty, and responsibility for the deterioration of a school.

Summary

It is a major responsibility of every administrator to ensure that each child is taught by a competent teacher. Administrators must have the knowledge and skills to assist teachers and classified staff to perform in a competent fashion. However, they also have an obligation to take disciplinary action when staff performance is unsatisfactory. The effective administrator must be well versed in progressive discipline, as well as the legal procedures and requirements to dismiss an employee when progressive discipline has not been effective.

Key Terms

1. discipline
2. dismissal
3. letter of reprimand
4. liberty interest
5. moral turpitude
6. non-renewal
7. oral warning/conference
8. progressive discipline
9. probationary status
10. property interest
11. reduction in force
12. suspension with pay
13. tenure
14. unsatisfactory evaluation
15. written warning

Discussion / Essay Questions

1. Review the steps in the Progressive Employee Discipline Model.

2. Develop a strong argument for elimination of tenure.

3. What is the major difference between "non-renewal" and "dismissal"?

4. Review the twelve legal grounds for dismissal. Discuss the three that you think are the most serious.

5. Give examples of unsatisfactory performance and the rationale for dismissal of a teacher based on your examples.

6. Define "property interest" and "liberty interest." Which of the two do you feel would be most difficult for a district to defend if challenged in a lawsuit?

7. Define "Reduction in Force." When is this method of staff dismissal justified?

References

Andelson, S. J. (1995). *FRISK documentation model.* Torrance, CA: Four Star Printing & Graphics.

Black's Law Dictionary (7th ed.). (1999). Bryan A. Garner, Editor-in-Chief. St. Paul, MN: West Group.

Bragdon, H. W., & McCutchen, S. E. (1961). *History of a free people.* New York: Macmillan.

Deskbook Encyclopedia of American School Law (1992). Rosemount, MN: Data Research.

Hartmeister, F. (1995). *Surviving as a teacher: The legal dimension.* Chicago, IL: Precept Press.

Jones, J. J., & Stout, I. W. (1960). *School public relations: Issues and cases.* New York: G. P. Putnam and Sons.

National Education Association. (1936). *A handbook on teacher tenure* (Research Bulletin 14). The author.

Rebore, R. W. (1998). *Personnel administration in education* (5th ed.). Boston, MA: Allyn and Bacon.

Ruud, R. C., & Woodford, J. J. (1992). *Supervisor's guide to documentation and file building for employee discipline.* Crestline CA: Advisory Publishing.

Court Cases

Adler v. Board of Education, 342, U.S. 485 (1952)

Roth v. Board of Regents, 408 U.S. 564 (1972)

Teachers Tenure Act Cases, 329 Pa. 213, 197 A. 344 (1938)

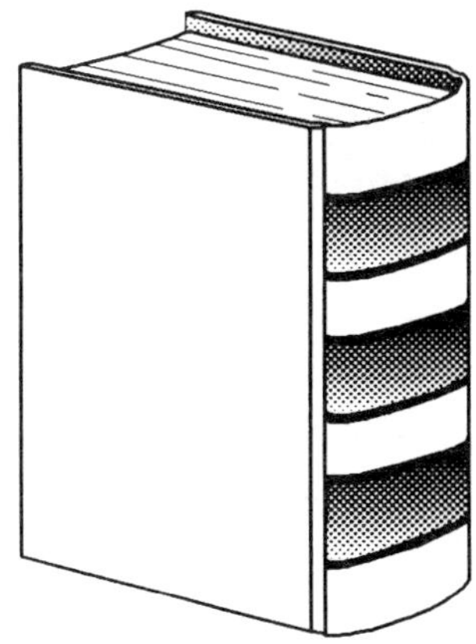

Chapter 9

Religion and the Schools

Introduction

From Colonial days until the mid-20th century, religious observances were prevalent in many public schools (McCarthy, Cambron-McCabe, & Thomas, 1998). However, since World War II, issues concerning church-state relations have provided a steady stream of litigation. No other area in school law, with the exception of school desegregation, has received more attention in the courts than issues involving religion in the public schools (Lunenburg, 1996).

The U.S. Constitution contains a provision that establishes the separation of church and state. This provision guarantees religious freedom on the one hand, and on the other, forbids an establishment of religion by the government. The First Amendment states that "Congress shall make no law respecting the establishment of religion, or prohibiting the free exercise thereof." These two religion clauses, the Establishment Clause and the Free Exercise Clause, protect an individual's religious liberty. The two clauses prohibit religious indoctrination in the public schools or use of public funds to support religion.

While most Americans accept the principle that public schools should be free of religious indoctrination, the issue does not end there. For example, in a presidential election year, each candidate emphasizes his support of prayer and family values. However, when pushed for specifics of his or her position on the separation of religion and schools, the candidate is usually vague on details. He or she might opt for a "silent moment of meditation" before an elementary class begins or mention the need for private, silent prayer prior to taking an exam.

During the 2u000 presidential campaign, Republican candidates found themselves facing questions about their beliefs on the creation of the universe. This dilemma was posed after the Kansas Board of Education adopted new testing standards that played down the scientific importance of evolution. The leading candidates agreed that decisions on curricula should be left to local schools.

When interviewed on CBS Face the Nation in August 1999, Elizabeth Dole said three times that she is a "person of strong faith," twice side-stepped the question of her beliefs about evolution, and concluded that such matters should be decided by the states (Schieffer, 1999). According to a Reuters press release (November 4, 1999) then-Texas Governor George W. Bush said local school districts should make their own decisions about what they teach. These examples reveal the conflict in American attitudes about the place of prayer and religion in the public schools.

This chapter addresses the Establishment Clause of the First Amendment to the Constitution, the constitutionality of daily Bible readings, prayers at graduation ceremonies, celebration of religious holidays, teaching of evolution, equal access in classrooms, separate religious public schools, and distribution of religious materials. Before studying the issues, it is important to understand how the separation of church and state came about through the influence of Thomas Jefferson.

Influence of Jefferson on the Separation of Church and State

Jefferson was very much influenced by the 18th-century movement called "Enlightenment." The dominant spirit of the century was one of skepticism toward all received truth. This spirit permeates Jefferson's work and thought. Jefferson came to prominence in 1776, when he participated in the General Assembly of the newly established Commonwealth of Virginia (Peterson, 1998).

During its early years the Church of England had been established in the Commonwealth, one of six American colonies with an Anglican establishment. The parish was responsible for collecting taxes from individuals within the territory, regardless of the church affiliation of the taxpayer. A large part of this money was used to support the Anglican Church. Not surprisingly, dissenters protested the unfairness of a system that required them to give financial support to a church whose tenets were different from their own. The number of dissenters from this religion increased during the 18th century. By Jefferson's time, as many as two-thirds of the citizens of Virginia were dissenters from the established church.

Jefferson advocated absolute religious freedom within the colony. James Madison joined Jefferson in promoting toleration of religious freedom and, reacting to the domination of the Anglican Church, wrote the English Act of Toleration.

Under this act, Protestants were allowed to hold religious services, provided that their ministers and places of worship were registered with the government.

After the Declaration of Independence was signed, Presbyterians in Virginia protested to the Virginia legislature against the "church tax." The Virginia legislature then passed a bill exempting all dissenters and minority sect members from paying taxes to the Anglican Church. Thus was the stage set for the First Amendment.

School Prayer and Bible Reading

During America's early history many public schools began each day with a prayer and Bible reading. Three significant Court decisions disallowed this practice. The cases were *Engel v. Vitale* (1962), *School District of Abington Township v. Schempp* (1963), and *Lemon v. Kurtzman* (1971). The U.S. Supreme Court decided that the Establishment Clause prohibits states and the federal government from passing laws that aid a religion or prefer one to another.

Engel v. Vitale

In 1962 school prayer in public schools had its first judicial review. The New York Supreme Court struck down a state statute requiring recitation of a prayer in the public schools on the ground that it violated the Establishment Clause. The court stated, "The Establishment Clause, unlike the Free Exercise Clause, does not depend upon any showing of direct governmental compulsion and is violated by the enactment of laws which establish an official religion whether those laws operate directly to coerce non-observing individuals or not." The court further stated that "when the power, prestige and financial support of government is placed behind a particular religious belief, the indirect coercive pressure upon religious minorities to conform to the prevailing officially approved religion is plain."

School District of Abington Township v. Schempp

One year later, in 1963, the Pennsylvania Supreme Court declared unconstitutional a Pennsylvania statute requiring Bible reading and recitation of the Lord's Prayer. The statute required that ten verses be read from the Holy Bible at the opening of each school day. Children would be excused from the exercise if their parents so requested in writing. The plaintiffs were members of the Unitarian Church. They brought action seeking to enjoin the enforcement of the statute when this exercise was part of the school curriculum and conducted under the supervision of teachers employed by the schools. A transcript by Irons (1993) describes how the prayer system worked.

> Between 8:15 a.m. and 8:30 a.m. every school day, all the children are in their homerooms. There's a public address system in each of the rooms. At 8:15 a.m. the morning exercise starts. First, they have what's called an introduction, a 'fact for the day.' The teachers pull something out of the *World Almanac* to gain the attention of the children. . . . This exercise is followed by ten verses of the Bible, read without comment. The ten verses of the Bible are followed by the Lord's Prayer, which in turn is followed by the flag salute, which in turn is followed by the school announcements for the day. . . . Then there is conclusion, where the names of the students who made the announcements are given. . . . The program is by the students enrolled in the television and radio workshop, which is a regular course of the English department. There are about thirty students in this course and it's voluntary.

On June 17, 1963, the Pennsylvania Supreme Court ruled in favor of Roger and Donna Schempp who filed the suit. The court ruled that public schools should not use the Bible and prayer for classroom devotion. Part of the court decision read: "What our Constitution protects is the freedom of each of us, be he Jew or Agnostic, Christian or Atheist, Buddhist or Freethinker, to believe or disbelieve, to worship, to pray or keep silent, according to his own conscience, uncoerced and unrestrained by government." So it is clear that in 1962 (*Engel*) and in 1963 (*Schempp*), the two state supreme courts struck down Bible reading and prayers in the public schools as unconstitutional.

Lemon v. Kurtzman

In *Lemon v. Kurtzman* (1971), the U.S. Supreme Court made clear that the government must maintain a neutral stance toward religion, that is, it may neither advance nor hinder any religion. This case involved a state program designed to reimburse all private schools, including religious schools, for expenses of textbooks, materials, and salaries to teach nonreligious subjects. Basing its decision primarily on the two religion clauses in the First Amendment, the Court devised an entanglement test, a three-part test now known as "the *Lemon* Test," for determining whether a particular governmental action withstands an Establishment Clause challenge. The *Lemon* Test contains three sections:

1. Does the action have a secular purpose?
2. Does the action have an effect that neither advances nor impedes religion?
3. Does the action avoid excessive entanglement with religion?

Chief Justice Burger authored this decision. It was decided that any issue that failed any one of the three parts of the *Lemon* Test was unconstitutional. In summary, state aid to parochial schools through salary supplements and purchase of services constitutes impermissible entanglement between church and state. This three-factor test has been applied in most Establishment Clause cases.

Graduation Ceremonies and Public Events

Recent cases regarding school prayer have focused on the graduation ceremony and other public events. Participation on such occasions was regarded as voluntary. The schools argued that these devotional activities were traditional and ceremonial. Initially, the courts appeared less inclined to find a violation of the Establishment Clause in baccalaureate services and prayers during graduation ceremonies than as routine devotional activities during the school day. In the mid-1980s, however, lower courts began striking down graduation prayers under the Establishment Clause, and the Supreme Court followed this lead in the case of *Lee v. Weisman* (1992).

Lee v. Weisman

This case arose in a Rhode Island School District that had a policy permitting principals to invite clergy to deliver invocations and benedictions at middle and high school graduation ceremonies. In its decision, the U.S. Supreme Court declared that opening prayers at graduation ceremonies were inconsistent with the religion clauses of the First Amendment. The Court followed the standard set in *Engel* and *Abington* that the free exercise of religion does not supersede the fundamental limitations imposed by the Establishment Clause.

The Court determined that elementary and secondary schools should be particularly sensitive to institutionalized prayer. In addition, telling students that they could choose not to attend would be regarded as unfair to the student. The Court recognized that high school graduation is one of the most significant occasions in life and that missing the graduation ceremony would be a major loss to a student.

The Court noted that the First Amendment protects freedom of religion and freedom of speech by quite different mechanisms. Speech is protected by ensuring its full expression, even when the government participates. The method for protecting freedom of worship and freedom of conscience in religious matters is quite the reverse. In religious debate or expression, the government is not a prime participant, for the framers of the Constitution deemed religious establishment antithetical to the freedom of all. The Free Exercise Clause, therefore, embraces a freedom of conscience and worship that has close parallels in the speech provisions of the First Amendment, but the Establishment Clause is a specific prohibition on forms of state intervention in religious affairs. Such a prohibition has no precise counterpart in the speech provisions.

The explanation lies in the lesson from history that inspired the Establishment Clause: "A state-created orthodoxy puts at grave risk that freedom of belief and conscience that are the sole assurance that religious faith is real, not imposed." In *Lee v. Weisman*, Justice Souter, speaking for the Court majority, based his reasoning on the *Lemon* Test. He argued that public school prayers at public school graduations appear to endorse religion and are therefore unconstitutional. However, Justices Scalia, Rehnquist, White, and Thomas dissented from this opinion. Their view was that prayer at graduation ceremonies is an American tradition. The four dissenters stated in their opinions that the *Lemon* Test should be rejected in this situation and that traditional religious practices should be allowed during graduation ceremonies.

As it turned out, the Supreme Court's decision did not reduce devotional activities in public school graduations, but in some cases had the opposite effect. Negative reactions to the ruling led school principals, teachers, and students to find creative strategies for offering prayers in graduation ceremonies. The Supreme Court had noted a difference between government speech endorsing religion, which the Establishment Clause forbids, and private speech endorsing religion, which the Free Speech and Free Exercise clauses protect (McCarthy, Cambron-McCabe, & Thomas, 1998). Some school districts, consequently, responded to *Weisman* by designating the graduation ceremony a forum for student expression. On this basis, they gave students discretion to include devotional messages in their graduation speeches.

Jane Doe v. Galveston

In 1999 the Supreme Court agreed to revisit this issue. The case of a Galveston, Texas area high school gave the Supreme Court its first chance to rule directly on student-led prayers (*Santa Fe Independent School District vs. Doe*).

In 1992 the U.S. Court of Appeals in Texas had become the first to uphold student-led invocations or benedictions, but only on condition that the religious messages were "non-sectarian and non-proselytizing." Two students, known only as "Jane Does," challenged this policy in federal court as a violation of the separation of church and state. Siding with the dissenting students, the U.S. Fifth Circuit Court of Appeals ruled that the school district had gone too far. The ruling rejected student-led prayers over the public address system at football games. Furthermore, with respect to graduation ceremonies, overtly Christian prayers carry the danger of polarizing and politicizing an event intended to celebrate the students' academic achievements, wrote Judge Wiener.

The school district appealed to the U.S. Supreme Court, arguing that it should not have to censor the religious content from student speech. Then-Governor Bush, speaking for the state of Texas, filed a brief supporting the school district. This effort was joined by the states of Alabama, Colorado, Kansas, Louisiana, Mississippi, Nebraska, South Carolina, and Tennessee. Nevertheless, when the Supreme Court issued its decision in June 2000, public prayer before a sporting event was disallowed. Forbidden was a situation in which "the state affirmatively sponsors the particular religious practice of prayer."

Silent Meditation in Public Schools

Persistent litigation regarding prayer and Bible reading in the public schools continued in the lower courts during the 1960s and 70s. However, not until 1985 did a challenge to silent meditation reach the Supreme Court in *Wallace v. Jaffree*. The question was whether a moment of silence was permissible. The U.S. Supreme Court held that an Alabama court ruling that authorized a one-minute period of silence in public schools for "meditation or voluntary prayer" was unconstitutional.

Still open is the question of the constitutionality of a "moment of silence." As of 1998, more than one-half the states had laws permitting student meditation or silent prayer. These laws are being challenged in many states, and the outcome is uncertain.

Religious Holidays, Celebrations, and Symbols

According to Stephen L. Carter, in his text *The Culture of Disbelief* (1993), the Supreme Court's *Lemon* Test is inadequate to determine when the Establishment Clause has been violated. Carter's view is that squaring *Lemon*'s rules with the accepted usage of our society's civil religion often requires some creative thinking. For example, how can one justify the expenditure of government funds to provide armed forces chaplains? In addition, a sticky question has revolved around use of public funds during the Christmas season to build and maintain a crèche, which celebrates the birth of Jesus Christ.

The Supreme Court, in *Lynch v. Donnelly* (1984), upheld inclusion of a nativity scene in a holiday display that also included a Santa Claus, a Christmas tree, a reindeer, a clown, a teddy bear, and other holiday symbols. The Court held that the scene had a legitimate secular purpose, that of celebrating the Christmas holiday and depicting its origins. The Court further held that the display may have "pushed" the Christian religion, but that any such effect was indirect, remote, and incidental.

The most memorable case on this issue was *Allegheny County v. Greater Pittsburgh American Civil Liberties Union* (1989). In this case the Supreme Court ruled that a nativity scene in the county courthouse violated the Establishment Clause because it had the effect of endorsing religion. However, a similar case showed that cultural diversity might be an acceptable alternative to showing a religious celebration. An exhibit outside a city court building showing a Christmas tree, a Chanukah menorah, and a "salute to liberty" message from the mayor was Constitutional because it merely acknowledged cultural diversity and the different traditions for celebrating the holiday season.

Every year at Halloween several news stories surface regarding parent protests against this holiday. Specifically, some parents object to depicting witches, goblins, devils, and other characters that are associated in their minds with witchcraft and Satanism. However, Halloween has never been outlawed as a holiday, on the argument that it has no religious significance. On the other hand, in *Fox v. City of Los Angeles* (1978), the California Supreme Court held that erection of a cross, decidedly a symbol of Christianity, was a violation of government neutrality. The court concluded that both the California Constitution and the United States Constitution prohibited this display on the part of the city as furthering an establishment of religion.

Released Time for Religious Instruction

The practice of releasing public school students during regular school hours for religious instruction first began in Gary, Indiana, in 1914 (Alexander & Alexander, 2001). Since then, two Supreme Court cases have addressed the issue of released time for religious instruction. In *McCollum v. Board of Education* (1948) the Court invalidated a program in which religion classes were taught in the public schools. The Court declared that the use of tax-supported school facilities to promote religious instruction was clearly a violation of the First Amendment.

In the second case, *Zorach v. Clausen* (1952), the Court upheld an arrangement in which students were permitted to leave the school premises during the school day to receive religious instruction at various religious centers. The difference between *Zorach* and *McCollum* was that the *Zorach* case did not involve use of public school buildings or the direct use of public funds, nor were the instructors employed or paid by the district. Under such circumstances, student released time for religious instruction is common in many communities.

Teaching of Evolution/Creation Science

It has been well established by the Supreme Court that a school district must neither prohibit instruction about evolution nor require that the instruction of evolution be balanced with the instruction of "creation science." A teacher named Peloza filed a suit involving this topic against the Capistrano Unified School District in California *(Peloza v. Capistrano Unified,* 1994).

Peloza was a biology teacher who alleged that the district had violated his Constitutional rights under the Free Speech, Establishment, and Equal Protection clauses. He also charged that school district administrators had conspired to violate his rights by harassment and intimidation because of a "class-based animus against practicing Christians."

The United States Court of Appeals for the Ninth Circuit concluded that if the school district required the plaintiff to teach evolution only as a scientific theory, then summary judgment in favor of the district would be appropriate. This case suggests that school districts should review their science curriculum to ensure they can document that evolution is taught as a scientific theory. Moreover, the court stated that Peloza would violate the Establishment Clause if he were to discuss his religious beliefs with students on the school grounds during contract time. This case was appealed to the U.S. Supreme Court, which declined to review it, thus letting the decision stand.

Use of Facilities

It is common practice for school districts to permit student organizations to use school buildings during non-instructional time. A school district that allows access to its facilities for student activities may not close them to student groups desiring to use the facilities for religious discussion and worship. This requirement is included in the federal Equal Access Act, passed in 1984, which requires public secondary schools that receive federal financial assistance to allow religious clubs to meet on the same basis as other non-curriculum-related activities.

In 1990 the Supreme Court resolved some of the legal questions regarding this issue when it rendered a decision in *Board of Education of Westside Community Schools v. Mergens* (1990). The case was a result of a group of high school students having asked permission to form a club that would meet at the public school during non-instructional time to engage in Bible discussions, prayer, and fellowship. The Court decided that the school could not bar the religious club from non-curriculum-related student group meetings during non-instructional time. The Court reasoned that denial of a student-initiated religious club while a variety of other non-curriculum-related student groups were recognized was a violation of the Equal Access Act. The Court decided that even if a school district were to allow only one non-curriculum-related group to use its facilities, then the Equal Access Act is triggered.

The California Education Code (section 38134) establishes requirements for use of school property in the state. Nonprofit organizations and clubs or associations organized to promote youth and school activities must be given access to school facilities. Examples include Girl and Boy Scouts, Camp Fire Girls, parent/teacher associations, and school-community advisory councils.

School districts may charge an amount not to exceed their direct costs for use of school facilities to any group, including religious organizations that supervise sports league activities. For other uses by religious organizations, however, the district must charge at least the amount of direct costs. Where admission fees are charged or contributions are solicited and the net receipts are not expended for the welfare of the students of the district or for charitable purposes, the district is required to charge a fair rental value for use of the property.

Establishment of a Separate Religious School

In *Board of Education of Kiryas Joel v. Grumet* (1994) the Supreme Court, in a 6:3 decision, ruled unconstitutional a New York law establishing a separate school district for a group of Orthodox Hasidic Jews. A New York religious community of about 8,500 Satmar Hasidim, a sect of Orthodox Jews who came to the United States from Europe after the holocaust, settled in a part of the town of Monroe that later became the Village of Kiryas Joel. The Satmar Hasidim are a strict religious people who speak Yiddish as their primary language. They wear distinctive clothing and keep apart from the outside world. For this reason, they neither watch television, listen to the radio, nor read English-language newspapers. Their children are educated in private, sex-segregated, parochial schools, where boys are trained in the Torah and girls for a role in the home.

Since the Satmar children attended private schools, what gave rise to this lawsuit? The difficulty was that the private schools did not provide special services for handicapped students. After 1985, when court decisions in other cases forced the local school district to discontinue sending its special education teachers to an annex of one of the Satmar private schools, the parents of these children had either to send them to a public school or to keep them at home. In public schools, the treatment accorded these young people, clothed and trained differently from their peers, led the parents to seek another solution. In response, the New York legislature passed a law in 1989 to constitute the Village of Kiryas Joel as a separate school district. In signing Chapter 748 into law, Governor Cuomo said it was designed to solve the unique problems associated with providing special education for the children of the village. The New York State School Boards Association, however, challenged Chapter 748 as an unconstitutional establishment of religion.

The trial court ruled that the statute was unconstitutional, failing all three prongs of the *Lemon* Test. The case eventually reached the Supreme Court, which also ruled against the establishment of the school. Justice Souter wrote the majority opinion, citing the necessity of government neutrality with respect to religion. The written decision of the Court is notable in the sarcasm of the dissenting opinion, penned by Justice Scalia. In his dissent, Scalia berated Justice Souter and those who agreed with him for having "abandoned text and history as guides" and presenting a case that "could scarcely be weaker."

Religious Dress in the Classroom

Some teachers in the public school system have challenged their district's dress code by wearing religious dress in their classrooms. Court decisions in such cases, though few in number, have held for the right of the school district to impose dress codes on employees. The prohibition of religious dress was upheld to ensure religious neutrality in the public schools.

Compulsory Education and the Amish

The classic case regarding compulsory school attendance is *Wisconsin v. Yoder* (1972). In this situation, the Amish refused to send their children to public or private school after they had graduated from the eighth grade. The Court held that the law of compulsory education would substantially interfere with the practice of a legitimate religious belief and that, for the state interest to prevail, the necessity of overriding the Amish practices must be extremely strong.

Curricular and Religious Materials in Public Schools

If we were to categorize the numerous articles relating to church vs. school issues, we would find those involving school curricular materials the most common. Recent cases have involved textbooks that included poems or stories considered inappropriate by one group or another. Many of these stories concerned Halloween: specifically, tales about ghosts, goblins, witches, and vampires. Plaintiffs have argued that because these characters are not in keeping with the Christian faith, they should not appear in literature for the classroom.

In *Grove v. Mead School District No. 354* (1985), parents tried to force a school district to remove from its English curriculum the book *The Learning Tree*, by Gordon Parks. The central idea of the novel is racism as viewed by an adolescent boy from an African-American family. The parents of Cassie, a sophomore high school student, were concerned that the school was requiring their daughter to read a book that violated the family's religious beliefs by advocating secular humanism. As a result of this challenge to the district, the student was assigned an alternative book. By this action, the district avoided any charge of coercion. However, the court made clear that the primary effect of the book was secular, that is, not related to religion, and that it was an appropriate selection for "exposing students to different cultural attitudes and outlooks." Thus, the district was justified in retaining the book in the curriculum. On appeal, the U.S. Supreme Court declined to review this case, thus allowing the decision to stand.

The U.S. Supreme Court has not directly addressed distribution of religious literature in public schools, and lower courts have rendered a range of opinions, most often prohibiting religious sects from distributing materials to captive public school audiences. As early as 1955, California's Attorney General rendered an opinion that the distribution of free Bibles to school children was prohibited. Subsequently, in 1993, a court of appeals dealt with a situation in which members of the Gideons International talked about their organization, then offered students a Bible from a stack laid out on a table in the classroom. In *Berger v. Rensselaer Central School Corporation* the court determined that this practice was unconstitutional. The court felt that the children were a captive audience, not free to leave the classroom during the presentation—an inappropriate entanglement of religion and government.

These and other court cases might encourage abandoning of moral and religious teaching in the schools. However, some aspects of these subjects are appropriate in public education. The most recent (1995) edition of *Moral, Civic, and Ethical Education: Teaching About Religion, Promoting Responsible Attitudes and Behaviors, and Preventing and Responding to Hate Violence*, published by the California Department of Education, provides guidance in these areas.

Summary

Some of the most interesting litigation in the church-school controversy involves challenges to materials and curriculum in the schools; Bible reading, prayer, and meditation in the school or classroom; prayer at graduation and other school events; religious symbols and celebrations; expressions of freedom in religious dress and speech; and conflicts related to school facilities and compulsory attendance. More than two hundred years have passed since our forefathers established the concept of religious neutrality in public education. Nevertheless, issues that were wrestled with in the 1800s continue to surface.

Such controversies will continue to arise as long as we are a people of many groups and diverse religions. Even our Supreme Court justices are not of one mind on these issues. It is essential that all public school teachers and administrators demonstrate sensitivity to the beliefs and customs of religious and nonreligious groups. The effective administrator will keep well informed about court decisions and board policies that provide guidance in this important area.

Key Terms

1. Act of Toleration
2. compulsory education
3. Equal Access Act
4. Establishment Clause
5. Free Exercise Clause
6. *Lemon* Test

Discussion / Essay Questions

1. Is it consistent to allow prayer before sessions of Congress, yet not at school? Why or why not?

2. Search an index covering the last three years of your nearest major California newspaper. What are the three most commonly mentioned controversies involving church versus school? Why are these such a dilemma for our citizens?

3. Do we allow a moment of silent meditation for the students in our schools? How is this different from prayer spoken out loud?

4. What curricular materials are most often objected to by parents?

5. Use the Internet to find three sites (URLs) that provide information about school law related to religion.

References

Alexander, K., & Alexander, M. D. (2001). *American public school law* (5th ed.). Belmont, CA: West/Thomson Learning.

Carter, S.J. (1993). *Culture of disbelief.* New York: Doubleday.

Irons, P., & Guitton, S. (1993). *May it please the court.* New York: University Press.

Lunenburg, F. C. (1996). *Educational administration: Concepts and practices.* (2nd ed.). Belmont, CA: Wadsworth.

McCarthy, M. M., Cambron-McCabe, N. H., & Thomas, S. B. (1998.) *Public school law* (4th ed.). Needham Heights, MA: Allyn & Bacon.

Peterson, M.D. (1998). *The Jefferson image in the American mind.* New York: University Press of Virginia.

Schieffer, B. (1999, Aug. 15). Face the nation, CBS [transcript]. Retrieved March 10, 2001, from Electric Library on the World Wide Web: http://wwws.elibrary.com.

Court Cases

Allegheny County v. Greater Pittsburgh American Civil Liberties Union, 492 U.S. 573, 109 S.Ct. 3086 (1989)

Berger v. Rensselaer Central School Corporation, 982 F.2d, 1160 (7th Cir. 1993)

Board of Education of Kiryas Joel v. Grumet, U.S. 114 S.Ct. 2481, 129 L.Ed.2nd 546 (1994)

Board of Education of Westside Community Schools v. Mergens, 496 U.S. 226, 110 S.Ct. 2356, 10 L.Ed.2d 191 (1990)

Engel v. Vitale, 370 U.S. 421, 82 S.Ct. 1261 (1962)

Fox v. City of Los Angeles, 22 Cal.3d. 792, 150 Cal.Rptr. 867 (1978)

Grove v. Mead School District No. 354, 753 F.2d. 1528, 22 Ed. Law.Rptr. 1141 (9th Cir. 1985), cert.denied 106 S.Ct. 85

Lee v. Weisman, 505 U.S. 577, 112 S.Ct. 2649 (1992)

Lemon v. Kurtzman, 403 U.S. 602, 91 S.Ct.2105 (1971)

Lynch v. Donnelly, 465 U.S. 668, 104 S.Ct. 1395 (1984)

McCollum v. Board of Education, 333 U.S. 203, 68 S.Ct. 461, 91 L.Ed.2d 649 (1948)

Peloza v. Capistrano Unified School District, 37F.3d. 517, 94 Ed.Law.Rptr. 1159 (9th Cir. 1994)

Santa Fe Independent School District vs. Doe, 120 S.Ct. 2266 (2000)

School District of Abington Township v. Schempp, 374 U.S. 203, 1, 83 S.Ct. 1560, 10 L.Ed.2d 844 (1963)

Wallace v. Jaffree, 472, U.S. 38, 105 S.Ct. 2479 (1985)

Wisconsin v. Yoder, 406 U.S. 205,92, S.Ct. 1526 (1972)

Zorach v. Clausen, 343 U.S. 306, 72 S.Ct. 679 (1952)

. . . .

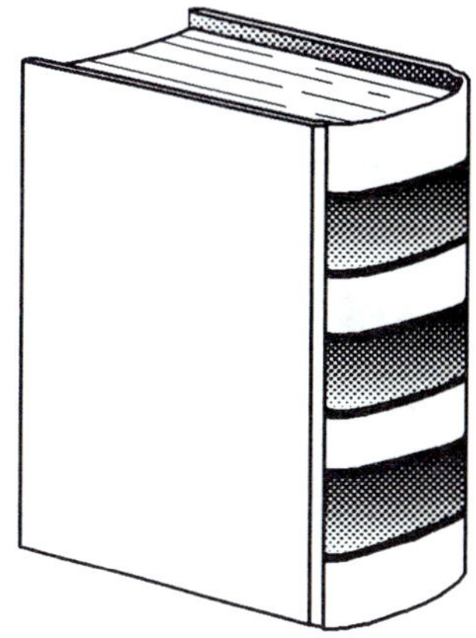

Chapter 10

School Finance and the Law

Introduction

For the first two centuries of the nation's history, local communities paid for public education. Today, public education is financed by a combination of state funds, local school district taxes, federal funds, and private grants. Since education is a function of state government, local school districts have limited power over their budgets. State control is particularly evident in California, where, in recent decades, the state has largely assumed responsibility for financing public education.

Education is big business—in many communities, the major source of employment. Education expenses also take a major bite out of most state budgets. In California, public education—kindergarten through community college—is guaranteed a minimum of 40% of the state budget. As a consequence, school finance is of extreme importance to taxpayers, the Governor, and the state legislature.

In addition to legislative controls over district revenues, the legislature exerts control by establishing rules for school board expenditures. State laws govern salaries, benefits, retirement contributions, and purchasing requirements. In addition, the law is very specific regarding a district's ability to tax and to borrow money.

Over the last several years, parents, taxpayers, and individual citizens have challenged the equality of financial support of schools at both state and national levels. This chapter provides a historical background for school finance and the major court decisions affecting school finance.

Financing Schools at the Local Level

Historically, states relied on local property taxes for the operation of school districts. However, as citizens became more aware of the disparities in per-pupil funding among districts, a movement was started to equalize funding by student.

Teachers, administrators, parents, and students have long recognized the difference in per-pupil expenditures from district to district. In two adjoining districts, one might be noted for excellent facilities, high paying salaries, and a generous supply of instructional materials, while the second district could have run-down facilities, a low salary schedule, and minimal instructional materials. Coupled with a desire to eliminate, or at least reduce, these inequalities, is a general recognition that equal resources do not ensure equal education. For example, children with exceptional needs caused by physical or mental handicaps may deserve extra funds.

The disparity in funding among districts gave rise in some states to legislation intended to mitigate such inequality. At the same time, several court cases were brought to force passage of just such laws. Plaintiffs charged that unequal spending for education was discriminatory and deprived students of their basic right to an adequate education. This argument did not succeed at the federal level and has not always fared well in the states, either.

Federal Challenges

The landmark case of *Brown v. Board of Education of Topeka* (1954) afforded the U.S. Supreme Court opportunity to rule on whether public education is a Constitutional right. The case was appealed to the Supreme Court by attorneys representing Linda Brown. Ms. Brown was an elementary school student in Topeka, Kansas, who was required to attend an all-black school when an all-white school was located much closer to her home.

Brown v. Topeka was a landmark case because it reversed an earlier decision of the U.S. Supreme Court in *Plessy v. Ferguson* (1896). In that decision the Court had approved the separate-but-equal doctrine. In *Brown*, however, the Court ruled that public education is a Constitutional right and that segregated schooling is inherently unequal. The decision addressed as critically important both opportunity for students to exchange views with students of different backgrounds and the inferiority feelings generated by separate schools. It was decided that in public education, the doctrine of separate-but-equal has no place.

State Challenges

The *Brown* recognition of education as a Constitutional right did not settle the question of equality in educational finance. That cause was taken up next at the state level. The first school finance cases asked whether states should allocate more funds to poor school districts and whether states were obligated to provide additional funds to educate students with special needs. Two state decisions helped establish legal precedents regarding school finance.

The first case was *Sawyer v. Gilmore* (1912), which challenged the school finance system in Maine. The plaintiff argued that Maine's distribution of school funds, which gave wealthier towns a larger proportion of funds, was unconstitutional. The court ruled that, although taxation might be equal and uniform, it did not necessarily follow that the benefits of that taxation must be distributed to all people in equal amounts.

The second case was *Dean v. Coddington* (1964). The South Dakota Supreme Court decided this case. The plaintiffs were taxpayers in a school district that did not have an elementary or secondary school. Therefore, the district did not receive funds from a foundation formula established by the legislature (Johns & Morphet, 1975). As in the *Sawyer* case, the court distinguished taxation from distribution, holding that the state's constitution did not require equal distribution of funds to all school districts. These two cases established the premise that the proportion of tax money collected by a state from residents of a school district need not be matched when funds are distributed back to the districts.

Equalization of Funding

Until the early part of the 20th century, state funding for schools was meager and typically was allocated on a flat per-pupil basis (Jordan, 1992). No adjustments were made for differences in the wealth of a district or the educational needs of its students. As early as the turn of the century, educators were advocating a system that would equalize funds to assist low-wealth districts.

The philosophical and legal arguments for equality of funding for education centered on four issues:

- Public education is a state function, not local.
- A child is a child of the state, not of the local school district.
- All school revenues are state revenues, regardless of whether they are collected at state or local levels.
- All school children are equal under the laws of the state.

Therefore, plaintiffs argued, the state could not combine state and local tax resources in such a manner as to benefit some children while ignoring needs of others (Alexander & Salmon, 1995). The plaintiffs presented the argument (later utilized in California's *Serrano* case) that a child's circumstances, that is, living in a poor district, should not determine the quality of his or her education.

Litigation proceeded in at least 23 states under the Equal Protection and Education clauses of state constitutions (Valente, 1998). Although the litigants were not very successful through the state courts in changing the system of financing local schools, they were able to promote legislation to equalize funding of education. Many states attempted to achieve this goal by utilizing other sources of revenue—state income tax, excise taxes, and fees—to support schools.

Perhaps the most successful case, *Rose v. Council for Better Education* (1989), was filed in a state court in Kentucky. The Kentucky Constitution states that the General Assembly shall, by appropriate legislation, provide for an efficient system of common schools throughout the state. The Kentucky Supreme Court examined the meaning of "an efficient system" by considering educational achievement. The court found that poorer districts were in greater need than richer districts. It concluded that Kentucky's funding system was underfunded and inadequate, as well as unequal and inequitable, and that educational funding must be increased and equitably distributed (Burrup, Brimley, & Garfield, 1993). This case broke new ground by overturning the state's entire education system—its organization, programs, structure, and governance. In this case the state's entire elementary and secondary education system was found in violation of the state constitution. To avoid dissolution of the entire system, the Kentucky legislature was forced, by a specified date, to pass legislation to meet the standards set by the court.

Odden and Wohlstetter (1992) report that as a result of a court mandate, or the threat of a mandate, more than 35 state legislatures enacted fundamental changes in their school finance structures between 1971 and 1985. These reforms had five major characteristics.

- They revamped the school finance equalization formula so as to send more state funds to property-poor, lower-spending districts.
- They increased the overall state role in funding schools.
- They increased state funding for special needs through compensatory, special, and bilingual education programs.
- The reforms increased aid for the extraordinary needs of large urban districts.

- Many reforms called for increased education taxes coupled with spending limitations that restricted local fiscal control over tax rates and curbed annual increases in expenditures per student.

California's *Serrano v. Priest*

Perhaps the best-known challenge to the method of funding local school districts occurred in California. What actually became a series of cases is referred to as *Serrano v. Priest*. This series occurred between 1971 and 1988. *Serrano I*, the first in the series, was initiated at the trial court level. The plaintiffs alleged that California's school finance system resulted in wide disparities in the revenue available to different school districts and violated the Equal Protection Clauses of the U.S. and California constitutions by making the quality of education dependent upon the wealth of a child's parents and geographical accident. They also contended that the system failed to take into account different educational needs of children in the various school districts. The defendants in the case, a group of county and state government officials, requested dismissal based on their contention that none of the stated facts were sufficient to constitute a cause of action.

The trial court ruled in favor of the defendants and granted the dismissal. The plaintiffs appealed that decision to the California Supreme Court. Since the appeal related to the dismissal order, rather than to a decision of the lower court, the court could not rule on the merits of the case. However, the California Supreme Court ruled that the plaintiffs had a basis for their claim. In this decision, the state supreme court noted that it had previously construed certain provisions of the California Constitution as equivalent to the Equal Protection Clause of the Fourteenth Amendment. The most important findings of the California Court were that "education is a fundamental right." The court gave five reasons in support of this view:

- Education is essential to preserving an individual's opportunity to compete successfully in the economic marketplace
- Education is universally relevant
- Few government services have as extensive contact with each recipient as does education
- Education is unmatched in the extent to which it molds the personality of the youth of society
- Education is so important that the state has made it compulsory.

After the California Supreme Court classified education as a fundamental right and determined that the state had not demonstrated that its funding system was adequate to the attainment of this compelling state interest, the case was remanded to the trial court, which then proceeded with a trial. The state legislature responded by changing the formula for financing public schools. In an attempt to equalize funding across districts, Senate Bill 90 was approved by the legislature and signed by the Governor. This legislation set a revenue limit—the maximum dollars per student in general-purpose state and local funds a district might receive. The key equalization feature was an adjustment that provided a higher dollar amount to low-revenue districts.

Next, *Serrano II* was brought to force a review of the new state school financial formula. The new procedure was found lacking. The court decreed that disparities between districts were too great and too slow in changing. However, in 1989, the California appellate court ruled that satisfactory progress had been made on equalizing expenditures between districts and closed the case.

The *Serrano* cases illustrate a major disadvantage confronted by plaintiffs who seek to use the courts as a means of changing public financing of schools. Litigation takes an inordinate amount of time. While *Serrano* did ultimately rule in the plaintiff's favor, the final decision took more than seven years.

It is interesting to note that, more than 25 years after the *Serrano* decision, disparities still exist among school districts in California. For example, in 1997-1998 the average per-pupil spending in unified districts across the state was $5,700. In Los Angeles County, however, the spending in unified districts ranged from $5,000 per pupil in Torrance to $7,050 in Beverly Hills. (These figures were adjusted to match the National Education Association definition. The data are available on the Internet at http://www.ed-data.k12.ca.us/)

San Antonio Independent School District v. Rodriguez

Between the time of *Serrano I* and *Serrano II*, the U.S. Supreme Court set an important precedent in *San Antonio Independent School District v. Rodriguez* (1973). This was the first case at the federal level relative to the disparities caused by utilizing local property taxes to finance education.

The plaintiffs in this case challenged the process for funding education in Texas, citing as their basis the Equal Protection Clause of the U.S. Constitution. Because the Texas system was similar to those in many other states, *Rodriguez* offered the Supreme Court an opportunity to force major restructuring of school funding systems across the country. An indication of the importance of this case is that 28 state attorney generals filed friend-of-the-court briefs, urging the Court to uphold the existing Texas funding system, which had been declared unconstitutional by a lower court.

The Court indicated that its test for determining whether a right is fundamental requires an assessment as to whether the right is explicitly or implicitly guaranteed by the Constitution. Contrary to the California decision in *Serrano,* the Court decided that since education is not mentioned in the Constitution, it is not among the rights afforded explicit protection. Consequently, the Court ruled in favor of the district and rejected the claim that the Texas form of taxation violated the Fourteenth Amendment's Equal Protection Clause. Nevertheless, although dismissing the argument that public education is a fundamental right, the Court acknowledged its historic dedication to public education and its abiding respect for the vital role of education in a free society. The Court declared that the state's system of taxation need only be rational to withstand Fourteenth Amendment challenges. This case, in effect, closed the federal court system as a route by which to challenge inequities in school finance.

Robinson v. Cahill

A series of seven separate court cases affecting education occurred in New Jersey between 1973 and 1976. The seven cases are referred to as *Robinson v. Cahill.* The first case was brought at the trial level; the court decided that the funding statutes in New Jersey violated the Equal Protection clauses of the U.S. and New Jersey constitutions. The decision was based on the fact that a high percentage of school revenue was generated from local taxation.

The trial court found that 67% of the statewide total school operating expenses came from local *ad valorem* taxation of real property, 28% from state appropriations, and 5% from federal aid (Jordan, 1992). As a result of this form of financial support for schools, a large disparity existed across districts in the amount spent per student. Therefore, the trial court held that the system unconstitutionally discriminated against students in low-wealth areas.

The New Jersey Supreme Court agreed that the system was unconstitutional, but for different reasons. The high court rejected the argument that a statewide uniformity in expenditure for education is required. The court suggested that local citizens could decide the amount of funds to be spent for education, much as they did for other services such as police and fire protection. Much like the *Rodriguez* court, New Jersey's Supreme Court rejected the argument that education is a fundamental right.

Turning to another issue, however, the court examined a clause in New Jersey's Constitution that required the legislature to provide for the maintenance and support of a thorough and efficient system of free public schools. The court decided that the state must define in some discernible way the educational obligation of school districts and compel each local district to raise the money necessary to provide that educational opportunity.

The Robinson case is important for educational finance in that a decision was made that the funding system was inconsistent with the state constitution on the basis of its Thorough and Efficient Clause, rather than under an equal protection clause. In addition, the details of the decision were more prescriptive in calling for remedies than previous court decisions had been.

Abbott v. Burke

It is interesting to note that the state of New Jersey, while near the top of all states in expenditures per student, again found itself in court in 1985. In this case, the New Jersey Public School Education Act was challenged as unconstitutional. The argument in *Abbott* was similar to that in *Robinson* in that the plaintiffs were students in schools located in poor districts. Attorneys for the students argued that the funding formula had not resulted in a thorough and efficient education for all New Jersey students. With the state contributing only 40% of all school operating costs, the majority of school funding was derived from local property taxes—an arrangement that still resulted in a sizeable funding disparity between high-wealth and low-wealth districts.

Like *Serrano*, *Abbott v. Burke* involved a long series of decisions. In the first case (1985), the New Jersey Supreme Court determined that the funding system under the Public School Education Act should be reviewed through administrative channels before the judicial system could rule on alleged constitutional problems.

After the administrative review was completed, the court issued its decision in *Abbott v. Burke II* (1990). The court declared the funding formula unconstitutional. The decision was again based on the Thorough and Efficient Clause of the state constitution. The court's ruling indicated that many decisions made in the field of education are based on the premise that the things money can buy affect the quality of education (Jordan, 1992). *Abbott V*, decided in May 1998, specified both funding and program requirements, the latter including full-day kindergarten and half-day pre-school, technology, and renovation of deficient facilities.

Edgewood Independent School District v. Kirby

Another state supreme court case, referred to as *Edgewood Independent School District v. Kirby* (1989), involved interpretation of the Texas State Constitution. This constitution contained a clause providing that since a general diffusion of knowledge is essential to the preservation of the liberties and rights of the people, it shall be the duty of the legislature of the state to establish and make suitable provision for the support and maintenance of an efficient system of public free schools. When the court reviewed the funding formulas across school districts, it found that the difference in property values was so great that the wealthiest district had more than $14 million of property wealth per student while the poorest had only $20,000, reflecting a 700 to 1 ratio. The court decided that general diffusion of knowledge meant knowledge spread statewide. It was decided that the funding formula was unconstitutional because it resulted in education that was limited and unbalanced, rather than a diffusion of education in general.

Ohio Supreme Court

A more recent state supreme court ruling came in Ohio in March, 1997. The Ohio court, by a four-to-three ruling, declared the state's system of funding education unconstitutional. The ruling was based on the concept of equalization of spending across districts. Ohio generates about half the money for public education from local taxes and about half from state revenues. As a result, because of differences in property values and wealth in each district, annual per-pupil spending ranged from $4,000 to $12,000 per student. The Ohio decision joins those of 12 other state supreme courts that have held that education is a fundamental right. Courts in nine other states have disagreed ("Ohio funding," 1997).

Williams et al. v. California (ACLU)

School finance issues in California are not yet settled. On May 17, 2000, the 46th anniversary of the decision in *Brown v. Board of Education*, the American Civil Liberties Union, with other organizations and individuals, filed a suit against the state of California alleging lack of instructional materials, too few credentialed teachers, overcrowded classrooms, and unhealthy conditions in eighteen districts in California. In September, the ACLU followed up with a motion asking the court to order the California Department of Education to institute a tracking system that would produce data as to the textbooks actually provided to districts in the state ("Back to School," 2000). In December, the state of California sued the eighteen districts, arguing that if their students lack adequate materials and facilities, the fault lies with the districts. In April 2001, the California School Board Association was granted permission to intervene in the case; CSBA spokespersons said that the organization was not entirely on either side, and on some points disagreed with both. At the same time the Superior Court Judge Busch, reversing an earlier decision, determined that the ACLU suit should be settled before the state's suit against the districts ("CSBA's motion," 2001). The case has been described as a "landmark case" and is certainly worth watching.

Summary

The citizens of the United States have repeatedly ranked education as the nation's number one priority. However, agreement on public education often stops there. Opinions vary widely as to what should be taught and how schools are to be financed. Moreover, great disparity is found in the financial support of education among the 50 states and individual districts within the states. Most states have attempted in some way to equalize the funding of education between wealthier and poorer districts. These attempts have in some cases been followed by lawsuits and court decisions.

It has not been easy for courts to wrestle with the societal problem of school funding and equalization of that funding. The courts tend to reflect the values and attitudes of a majority of the people toward the issues and questions on which they are ruling—values and attitudes that, with respect to school finance, have been changing. Until the early 1970s, higher courts refused to interfere or to rule in certain types of school finance cases. This position was based on the rationale that the methods used to collect and distribute funds to local school districts were a legislative, not a judicial, problem.

Serrano v. Priest (1971) brought a major change when California's Supreme Court set standards that overturned the state's system of financing schools. As a result of *Serrano*, almost every state made efforts to improve its method of financing education. Although *San Antonio Independent School District v. Rodriguez* (1973) effectively ended appeals to the federal courts, the school finance issue continues to be brought in state courts, and litigation will undoubtedly continue well into the early decades of the 21st century.

Key Terms

1. compelling state interest
2. education as a fundamental right
3. Equal Protection Clause
4. equalization
5. friend of the court
6. general diffusion of knowledge
7. property taxes
8. Senate Bill 90

Discussion / Essay Questions

1. *Brown v. Board of Education of Topeka* (1954) is hailed as a landmark Supreme Court decision. Discuss the important precedent that was established in this decision and the Court's rationale.

2. The majority of states have attempted to equalize funding among wealthier and poorer school districts. Discuss the steps that have been taken by state legislatures in their attempts to equalize school funding.

3. California's *Serrano v. Priest* (1988) decision had a profound effect on the financing of education in that state and many other states. How did this decision affect the financing of schools?

4. The U.S. Supreme Court in *San Antonio Independent School District v. Rodriguez* (1973) made a decision contrary to that reached in *Serrano v. Priest* (1988). Compare the two decisions. What was the rationale for each?

5. The concept of "Thorough and Efficient" was argued in *Abbott v. Burke* (1990). Where did this concept originate? How did the plaintiffs use it?

References

Alexander, K., & Salmon, R. (1995). *Public school finance.* Needham Heights, MA: Allyn & Bacon.

Back to school without books: Many CA students still lack textbooks, ACLU charges. (2000, September 12). ACLU Press Release. Retrieved from the World Wide Web March 19, 2001, from the World Wide Web: http://www.aclu.org/news/2000/n091200b.htm

Burrup, P. E., Brimley, V., & Garfield, R. R. (1993). *Financing education in a climate of change* (5th ed.). Needham Heights, MA: Allyn & Bacon.

CSBA's motion granted in school equity lawsuit. (2001, April 12). [CSBA Legal Notice]. Retrieved May 21, 2001, from the World Wide Web: http://www.csba.org/Communications/top_stories/headline3-29.htm

Johns, R. L., & Morphet, E. L. (1975). *The economics and financing of education: A systems approach.* Englewood Cliffs, NJ: Prentice Hall.

Jordan, K. F., & Lyons, T. S. (1992). *Financing public education in an era of change.* Bloomington, IN: Phi Delta Kappa Educational Foundation.

Odden, A., & Wohlstetter, P. (1992). The role of agenda-setting in the politics of school finance, 1970-1990. *Educational Policy, 4,* 355-376.

Ohio funding unconstitutional. (1997, March 25). *Orange County Register.*

Valente, W. D. (1998). *Law in the schools* (4th ed.). Upper Saddle River, NJ: Prentice Hall.

Court Cases

Abbott v. Burke, 100 N.J. 269, 495 A.2d 376 (1985), 119 N.J. 287, 575 A.2d 359 (1990), 153 N.J. 480, 710 A.2d 450; 1998 N.J. LEXIS 451 (1998)

Brown v. Board of Education of Topeka, 347 U.S. 483 (1954)

Dean v. Coddington, 81 S.D. 140, 131 N.W.2d 700 (1964)

Edgewood Independent School District v. Kirby, 777 S.W. 2d 391 (Tex. 1989)

Plessy v. Ferguson, 163 U.S. 537, 16 S.Ct. 1138 (1896)

Robinson v. Cahill, 62 N.J. 473, 303 A.2d 273 (1973), 70 N.J. 464, 306 A.2d. 457 (1976)

Rose v. Council for Better Education, Inc., 790 S.W. 2d 186 (Ky. 1989)

San Antonio Independent School District v. Rodriguez, 411 U.S. 1 (1973)

Sawyer v. Gilmore, 109 Me. 169, 83 A 673 (Me. 1912)

Serrano v. Priest, 487 P. 2nd 1241 (Cal. 1971), 557 P. 2d 929 (Cal. 1976), cert. den. 432 U.S. 907 (1977), rev. granted 763 P. 2d 852 (Cal. 1988)

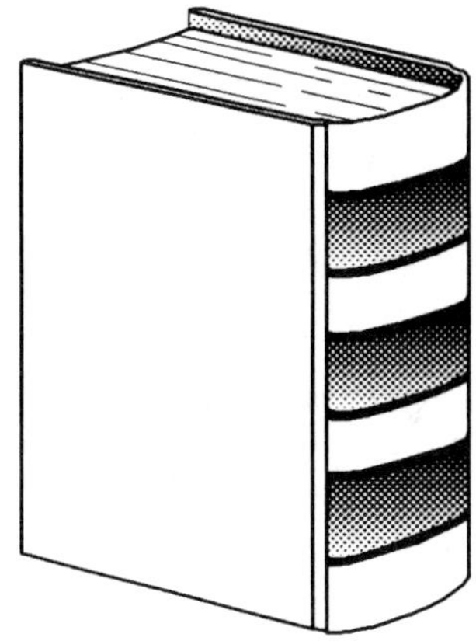

Chapter 11

Copyright Law and Education

Introduction

Breaking copyright, patent, or trademark law in the United States can be serious business. Consider what happened a couple of years ago when the Academy Awards ceremony in Los Angeles featured a dance by a man dressed up as Snow White! No one on the production staff had thought about obtaining permission from the Walt Disney company to present this spoof. However, Walt's heirs, not finding the dancing Snow White at all funny, slapped a multimillion dollar suit on the producers of Academy Awards.

More recently, the concern for intellectual ownership has been demonstrated as writers, composers, producers, and other originators file lawsuits in an attempt to protect their creative endeavors. School districts and individual educators have been the defendants in some of these suits. This fact, combined with the contributions of technology in simplifying the copying of both print and nonprint materials, has made copyright infringement a major concern to teachers. This chapter provides the teacher and administrator with a brief history of copyright law and information about significant court cases regarding copyright infringement. A review of permissible and prohibited use of copyrighted materials in schools is also included.

Copyright Terms

The legal structure that governs rules of ownership has developed its own language, and it is important to differentiate between some commonly used terms. The following definitions are drawn from *Black's Law Dictionary* (1999), except as indicated.

Copyright: A property right in an original work of authorship (such as literary, musical, artistic, photographic, or film work) fixed in any tangible medium of expression, giving the holder the exclusive right to reproduce, adapt, distribute, perform, and display the work.

Copyright Notice: A necessary notice in the form required by law that is placed in each published copy of a work. All copies of a product should include the name of the owner of the copyright, the year of first publication, and either the copyright symbol (©) or the word "copyright" (Fischer, Schimmel, & Kelly, 1995).

Fair Use Doctrine: A reasonable and limited use of a copyrighted work without the author's permission. Factors affecting the application of the definition include the purpose and character of the use, the nature of the copyrighted work, the amount of the work used, and the economic impact of the use. The Copyright Office of the Library of Congress publishes a guide to fair use for educators and librarians ("Reproduction," 1995).

Patent: The exclusive right to make, use, or sell an invention for a specified period, usually seventeen years.

Plagiarism: The act or an instance of copying or stealing another person's words or ideas and attributing them as one's own. *Black's* cites Goldstein (1994) on the point that plagiarism is an ethical offense, applying both to copyrighted works and works in the public domain. If the material plagiarized is under copyright, then the plagiarism is also illegal.

Public Domain: A work enters the public domain upon expiration of the copyright; this is the case for materials first published 75 or more years ago. Additional works usually in the public domain are those published before 1978 without copyright notice and those published without copyright notice between January 1, 1978, and March 1, 1989, and then not registered within five years (Leaffer, 1998).

Trademark: A word, phrase, logo, or other graphic symbol used by a manufacturer or seller to distinguish its product or products from those of others.

Historical Context of Copyright Law

It was in 1476 that the printing press was introduced into England and became the tool for large-scale reproduction of books (Leaffer, 1998). The printed word caused problems for the English leadership, as it gave critics an opportunity to be heard.

Under English law at that time, companies were allowed to publish manuscripts under the "protection" of the Crown. In effect, this practice allowed the government to censor all printed materials. However, even at that time, some enterprising companies copied materials without the Crown's protection.

As printing became more common and questions about authorship continued to surface, the English Parliament responded by adopting the Statute of Anne in 1709. For the first time, the right of authors was established. Under this law, authors were given ownership of their work for two 14-year terms (Foster & Shook, 1993).

Congress first enacted copyright legislation in 1790. Revisions occurred twice during the 19th century. However, the first comprehensive copyright law approved in the United States was the Copyright Act of 1909. This act expanded copyrightable subject matter to all works of an author. In addition, the law created a longer term of copyright protection: two terms of 28 years each.

International copyright has also been a concern. The Berne Convention of 1886 established mutual copyright protection among signatory nations. In these countries, copyright registration in any member nation is recognized.

The Copyright Act of 1976

It was not until 1976 that Congress approved legislation that set specific guidelines for copyright protection. The Copyright Act of that year was designed to clarify the copyright legislation approved in 1909. The new law extended the length of years for copyright protection and attempted to clarify what items might be subject to copyright protection. Under this act:

- Copyright is wholly under federal jurisdiction, rather than a dual system involving both state and federal governments.
- All works with a tangible medium of expression are protected from the moment of creation.

- Length of protection, formerly 28 years and renewable, extends to the life of the author plus 50 years.
- Copyright protection, originally granted only to books, maps, and charts, has been extended over the years to include musical compositions, graphic works, photographs and motion pictures, digital technology, and multimedia productions (*Patry,* 1994, as cited in *Black's Law Dictionary*, 1999).

The new legislation moved toward codifying the concept of "fair use," which includes flexibility for teachers to use copyrighted materials in the classroom under specified conditions.

An Author's Exclusive Rights

The 1976 law outlined the rights of authors. The owner of a copyright has the exclusive right to do and to authorize any of the following:

- reproduction of the work in copies or phonorecords
- preparation of derivative works based upon the copyrighted works
- distribution to the public of copies or phonorecords, whether by sale or other transfer of ownership, or by rental, lease, or loan
- public performance or presentation of literary, musical, dramatic, choreographic, or audiovisual works, or of pantomimes or motion pictures
- public display of literary, musical, dramatic, choreographic, graphic, pictorial, or audiovisual works, or of pantomimes, sculptures, or individual images from a motion picture or other audiovisual work (Title 17, U.S.C. section 106)

The Doctrine of Fair Use

The right of authors to control their work is offset by the need of society to have ready access to those same works. Guidelines to balance these conflicting interests fall within the doctrine of fair use. Of particular interest to educators are privileges allowed for scholarly work and for teaching. Helpful publications for this purpose are Copyright Circular 21, "Reproduction of Copyrighted Works by Educators and Librarians" (1995) and a recent publication of Phi Delta Kappa

International, *An Educator's Guide to Finding Resources in the Public Domain* (Potter, 1999).

The Four Criteria

The most important point regarding fair use is the four criteria to be applied:

- the purpose and character of the use, including commercial use versus nonprofit, educational purposes
- the nature of the copyrighted work
- the length of the portion used in relation to the copyrighted work as a whole, and
- the effect of the use upon the potential market for or value of the copyrighted work.

In addition to the four criteria above, unofficial photocopy guidelines were prepared for educators in connection with the revision of 1976. The text of these guidelines appeared in a House of Representatives report and is available in Copyright Circular 21 ("Reproduction," 1995).

According to these guidelines, a single copy may be made by or for a teacher for the teacher's scholarly research or use in teaching or preparation to teach a class. The limit for single copies includes:

- a chapter from a book
- an article from a periodical or newspaper
- a short story, short essay or short poem
- a chart, graph, diagram, drawing, cartoon or picture from a book, periodical, or newspaper

Although the guidelines permit single copies of copyrighted material for teaching or research, they are quite restrictive as to multiple copies. Up to one copy per pupil may be made if the situation meets three tests: brevity, spontaneity, *and* cumulative effect ("Reproduction," 1995). The guidelines for these tests are, in part, as follows:

Brevity: In prose, limited to a complete article, story, or essay of less than 2,500 words or an excerpt from any prose work of not more than 1,000 words or 10% of the work, whichever is less.

Spontaneity: Initiated at the discretion and inspiration of the individual teacher and with so short a time between the decision to use the material and the effective time of its use that it would be unreasonable to expect a timely reply to a request for permission.

Cumulative Effect: Copied for only one course in the school; and except for current news, limited in one class term to one short poem, article, story, essay or two excerpts from a single author; three items from the same collective work or periodical volume; for a total of nine instances of such multiple copying for one course during one class term.

Prohibited Uses of Materials

There are several prohibitions with respect to fair use:

- Copying may not be used to create or replace anthologies.
- There may be no copying from works intended to be consumable, such as standardized answer sheets.
- Copying may not substitute for the purchase of the books.
- The same teacher may not repeat copying the same item in a subsequent term.
- Students may not be charged more than the actual cost of photocopying the material.

Libraries

Fair use privileges also extend to libraries, which may make a single copy of a copyrighted work. The primary purpose of the copy may not involve commercial advantage. If a library allows photocopying of materials, it must do so on the premise that the copy becomes the property of the user. The library must have no knowledge that the copy would be used for any other purpose other than private study, scholarship, or research. In addition, the library must prominently display in the copy area a warning against inappropriate duplication of copyrighted material.

Performance or Display of a Work

Performance or display of a work by instructors of pupils is not an infringement, even if pupils act out the work. However, the performance must be part of systematic instructional activities, as well as directly related and of material assistance to the teaching process. The performance may not serve as recreation or entertainment for any part of the audience. It cannot be broadcast by radio or television unless primarily for reception in the classroom by students whose disabilities prohibit their attendance at the performance or for reception by a governmental employee as part of official duty.

Off-Air Taping of Television Programs

Many teachers tape radio broadcasts or television programs for later showing to students. This taping may constitute copyright infringement if off-the-air-taping guidelines are not followed. In 1979 representatives of education and the producers worked with a House of Representatives committee to develop "Guidelines for Off-Air Recording of Broadcast Programming for Educational Purposes." Essential excerpts from this report are included in Circular 21 from the U.S. Copyright Office ("Reproduction," 1995). Libraries may not keep videotapes for distribution to teachers, and educational institutions are expected to establish appropriate control procedures to ensure implementation of the off-the-air guidelines.

The U.S. Supreme Court addressed this issue in 1984 in the case *Sony Corporation v. Universal City Studios.* The Court upheld "time-shifting," that is taping a program to view at a more convenient time. The taped material may be used only for relevant classroom activities and only once within the first 10 days of taping. Additional use is limited to instructional review or student testing. After 45 days the tape must be erased.

Educational Use of Music

For academic purposes other than performance, up to one copy per pupil may be made of short excerpts from a musical work, but not enough to make up a performable section. Emergency copying for a performance is also allowed, on condition that the photocopies are subsequently replaced with purchased originals. Details are included in Copyright Circular 21 ("Reproduction," 1995).

Copying of Computer Software

Illegal copying of computer software by school personnel concerns programmers and publishers. Limited school budgets combined with the high cost of software create a temptation for teachers to share programs—a practice that constitutes copyright abuse. The copyright law was amended in 1980 to reflect the increasing use of educational software. It is clear from the amended law that a teacher may make only one duplicate or backup copy of the master computer program.

A fundamental principle of copyright law is that the copyright protects forms of expression, and not the ideas that are expressed (Keplinger, 1981). In keeping with this principle, a copyright does not protect the algorithm, or underlying process, upon which a computer program is based. Such protection should be obtained under the laws governing patents, in which the determining standard is novelty.

Case Law Regarding Fair Use

Recognition of the value of creative works and concern for copyright protection has resulted in several court cases. One of the most publicized was brought against Kinko's Inc., a company that specializes in copying services.

Basic Books v. Kinko's Graphic Corp.

The *Kinko's* case (*Basic Books Inc. v. Kinko's Graphics Corp.*, 1991) resulted from that company's practice of preparing instructor course materials designed for sale to students. These packets were compiled from texts and articles. The lawsuit involved eight publishing companies that sued Kinko's copy centers, alleging infringement of the Copyright Act. The plaintiffs charged that Kinko's had copied excerpts of many copyrighted books, then turned the excerpts into packets to be sold to students at a profit (Kasunic, 1992). Kinko's countered that although the packets were a profit-making venture, the material was educational in content and served an educational purpose. Therefore, Kinko's argued, the practice fell within fair use.

The court ruled that copyright permission must be obtained if packets of materials are to be sold to students on a profit basis. After weighing the fair-use factors, the courts found for the publishing companies. Their logic was that even though the photocopied material had an educational purpose, Kinko's was a commercial enterprise making a profit on the materials. The courts applied the four criteria of fair use and found that economic benefits were accruing to Kinko's Copy, Inc.

This case has caused a great deal of confusion, since many educators and educational institutions overreacted, creating rules that went beyond the limitations suggested by the court. Many campus bookstores became reluctant to copy materials assembled by college instructors and designed for sale to students. It should be remembered that the intent of the copyright law is to provide a balance between educational and cultural progress on the one hand, and an author's incentive to create works that will yield exclusive benefit, on the other. Although copyright clearance *is* important in assembling student packets, a number of companies now offer a service that includes obtaining copyright clearance for such materials. In addition, many schools and libraries work with the Copyright Clearance Center for this purpose. An individual faculty may also contact the copyright holder by mail or e-mail to request permission to reproduce materials for educational purposes. The request must specify the material to be copied, the number of copies to be made, and the purpose. The copyright holder may require a fee for reproduction in books or other publications.

Campbell v. Acuff-Rose Music

A case involving musical material was *Campbell v. Acuff-Rose Music* (1994). In this case, Acuff-Rose Music Company owned the copyright to Roy Orbison's 1964 hit song, "Oh, Pretty Woman." The rap group 2 Live Crew recorded a satirical version, using the same drumbeat and bass line, repeated eight times throughout the song. They substituted words such as "two-timin' woman," "bald-headed woman," and "big, hairy woman," for the original lyrics. The Supreme Court held that a commercial parody may qualify as fair use. It was decided that a parody's "transformative" character is more important than its commercial purpose. The test question asks whether the new effort alters the original with a new "message, meaning and expression." In the decision of the Court, the parody assumed this transformative spirit.

Other Cases

One interesting case that creates a context for fair use law is the case of *Wihtol v. Crow* (1962). In this case the defendant, a music professor, created a new arrangement of a copyrighted hymn (Kasunic, 1992). Since the professor directed the choir at school and church, he made 48 copies of the hymn for his choir. He then attempted to sell the new arrangement to the plaintiff's publisher. The court held that the defendant violated the concept of fair use. The copyright owner earned about $25,000 annually in royalties and licenses, and the professor's action had potential to affect the plaintiff's income.

Another case involved a professor and the author of a copyrighted cake-decorating textbook (Kasunic, 1992). The defendant had attended the professor's class and created another cake-decorating book, which she distributed to a class she taught. She used 11 of the plaintiff's 29 pages, but failed to attribute any of these pages to the plaintiff. The court of appeals found that the use of the copyrighted work did not meet the tests of fair use. What made an impression on this court were the facts that, first, the defendant did not credit the copyright holder at all in the new text and, second, that the copied pages were such a substantial part of the new work.

It is obvious from the changes in law during the past several years that the pendulum has swung toward giving authors more power to control their works. The

United States is very much in the "information age," rather than the "industrial age." Therefore, many questions involving copyright laws are still unanswered.

Summary

"Intellectual property" is important in a technological society such as the United States. It is important to remember that it is the "use" of the property that is significant. Educators are interested primarily in "fair use." If they make limited numbers of copies and do so spontaneously and with scholarly or educational intent, then there should be no issue. If the original work is altered and authorship is claimed by another, then the courts have intervened to determine who should be deemed owner of the work. As the Internet assumes more significance, questions of copyright protection and infringement will certainly increase in importance and complexity.

Key Terms

1. copyright
2. Copyright Law of 1976
3. copyright notice
4. fair use
5. patent law
6. public domain
7. trademark
8. trademark law

Discussion / Essay Questions

1. If a teacher wants to make 30 copies for her class of a current newspaper article, should she take any precautions with regard to the copyright law?

2. Can you make a copy of a computer program for a friend? Why or why not?

3. What are the four criteria that one should apply to determine whether use of copyrighted material falls under "fair use"?

4. With respect to videotaping of a television program, what is the meaning of "time-shifting"?

5. Make a list of prohibited copying practices.

References

Black's Law Dictionary (7th ed.). (1999). Bryan A. Garner, Editor-in-Chief. St. Paul, MN: West Group.

Fisher, L., Schimmel, D., & Kelly, C. (1995). *Teachers and the law* (4th ed.). White Plains, NY: Longman.

Foster, F. H., & Shook, R. L. (1993). Patents, copyrights, & trademarks (2nd ed.). New York: John Wiley.

Kasunic, R. (1992). Fair use and the educator's right to photocopy copyrighted material for classroom use. *Journal of College and University Law, 19*, 271-273.

Keplinger, M. S. (1981). Computer software—its nature and its protection. *Emory Law Journal, 30*, 483-485.

Leaffer, M. (1995). *Understanding copyright law.* New York: Times Mirror Books.

Potter, K. D. (1999). *An educator's guide to finding resources in the public domain.* Bloomington, IN: Phi Delta Kappa International.

Reproduction of copyrighted works by educators and librarians. (1995). Washington, DC: Copyright Office, Library of Congress. Available on the World Wide Web at http://www.loc.gov/copyright/ circs/circ21.pdf

Court Cases

Basic Books Inc. v. Kinko's Graphics Corp., 758 F. supp. 1522 S.D.N.Y. (1991)

Campbell v. Acuff-Rose Music Inc., 114 S.Ct. 1164 (1994)

Sony Corporation v. Universal City Studios, 465 U.S. 1112, 104 S.Ct. 1619 (1984)

Wihtol v. Crow, 309 F 2d 777 (8th Cir. 1962)

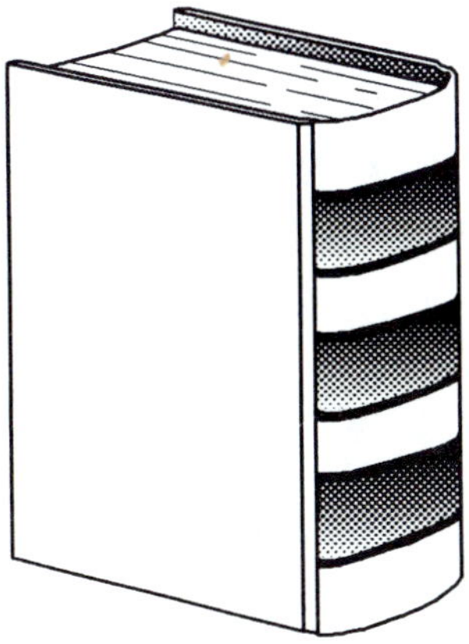

Chapter 12

Tort Liability in Schools and Districts

Introduction

Xavier Castro, a 14-year-old student at Colton High School in California, was shot to death on his way home from school on May 22, 1996. The shooting occurred at about 2:20 p.m. as Xavier and two friends were headed to Kentucky Fried Chicken. A gunman began shooting at them. A bullet caught Xavier in the leg and, as he lay wounded, the attacker moved closer and shot Xavier in the head. Xavier's mother filed a $2 million wrongful death claim against the Colton School District, charging that the district failed to exercise the proper standard of care for supervising students. Does Xavier's mother have a case?

Let's examine some additional information. The alleged attacker, Ascención Gomez, had been expelled from the Colton district for an act of violence on campus. Although Ascención had been expelled, and district policy forbids students to be on campus when expelled, Ascención had sat in a Spanish teacher's class just prior to the shooting. The teacher, Edda Osaba, said she was with Gomez immediately before and after the time of the shooting. Osaba said she offered to give Gomez books to read during the summer and offered him a ride home in her car after school, although it is against school policy to drive students in personal vehicles. Does Xavier's mother now have stronger case?

In 1996 a Contra Costa Superior Court Jury awarded $500,000 to a girl who was harassed by a sixth-grade classmate. The harassment included vulgar acts directed at her, lewd insults about the girl's body, and threats to beat her up and kill her. The jury based its decision on evidence that the district had failed to stop the harassment.

Both children were sixth-graders at Bidwell Elementary School in Antioch. The parents had met with the teacher, principal, the boy's family, and the superintendent. The harassment continued. The superintendent said the parents had not had sufficient evidence to justify moving the boy to another class or for suspending him. "It's an unfortunate circumstance that we found ourselves in the middle of," Superintendent Alan Newell said. "We clearly have a social issue which, as a society, we're going to have to address." Negligence charges against Newell were dropped after Judge Ingazio Ruvolo ruled that the family did not have enough evidence to hold him personally responsible (Irvine, 1996).

Is the shooting of Xavier just an isolated incident of violence on school campuses? The answer is a resounding "No." Are lawsuits often filed against school districts? The answer this time is an equally strong "Yes."

Consider the statistics: In 1982 a joint powers agreement was formed in San Bernardino and Riverside Counties to provide insurance coverage for 35 school districts. During its first fourteen years, the agency, now the Southern California Schools Risk Management Authority, received 4,053 claims, for a total in excess of $31 million. The largest number of claims fell into category 337, miscellaneous auto accidents, followed by accidents in physical education and athletics (category 299) and theft of property (256). The largest dollar amounts were for injuries in physical education and athletics ($5,220,699) and injuries suffered by students on the playground ($4,130,083) (Inland Empire Insurance Authority, 1996).

As the number and size of claims against school districts demonstrate, to provide a safe environment for children must be a district's number one priority. Teachers, administrators, school board members, and all school district employees have a duty to provide a safe environment for students at school or when involved in school-related activities. In 1982 the California Constitution was amended to require that "all students and staff of public primary, elementary, junior high, and senior high schools have the inalienable right to attend campuses that are safe, secure, and peaceful" (Article I, Section 28 c). This amendment builds on compulsory attendance, the legal requirement that children attend school.

Administrators and teachers have good reason to be concerned about liability while students are under their care. Although a school district is not expected to guarantee that no child will ever be hurt, school employees are expected to exercise the same standard of care that a reasonably prudent parent would have exercised under the same or similar circumstances. Thus, an employee may be personally liable for monetary damages if his or her actions and conduct fail to satisfy the standard of appropriate care.

In one case, a gay student who was beaten and tormented in school was awarded $900,000 by a Wisconsin jury. The principal and two assistant principals were held personally liable for not having provided an appropriate, safe school environment for the student. This case led to the first federal trial of a school district for not protecting a gay student from harassment ("School settles," 1996).

Under state tort law, each individual is granted certain rights that other persons must respect. If an individual fails to respect these rights and, in consequence, damages another person, a tort has been committed, and the offending party may be held liable. This chapter provides a definition of torts and a discussion of the various types of torts. Included are examples of tort lawsuits against districts and employees, with suggested precautions to avoid tort liability. The chapter also outlines the damages most commonly sought by plaintiffs in a civil lawsuit for tort.

Torts Defined

A tort is not a crime, but comes from a separate and distinct body of law known as "civil law." Civil lawsuits pertain to the private rights of citizens, whereas criminal trials are initiated by the state to identify and punish those who have committed public offenses. Criminal proceedings are also intended to protect the public from actions of a wrongdoer. In a criminal case the state prosecutes, not to compensate the injured person, but rather to protect the public from further wrongful acts. Since criminal law does not compensate an injured individual, social justice demanded another avenue through which an injured party might obtain redress. Thus, tort actions became a legal tool.

Tort cases primarily involve state law and are grounded in the fundamental premise that all individuals are liable for the consequences of conduct that results in injury to others. "Tort" is defined as a civil wrong, other than breach of contract, for which a court may provide relief in the form of monetary damages. According to *Webster's Dictionary*, the word "tort" is derived from the Latin word "tortus," meaning "twisted." *Black's Law Dictionary* (1999) defines "tort" as "a civil wrong for which a remedy may be obtained, usually in the form of damages; a breach of duty that the law imposes on everyone in the same relation to one another as those involved in a given transaction." Tort law applies to school districts, school officers, and school employees.

Types of Torts

Tort actions are grouped into five major categories: intentional, strict liability, educational malpractice, constitutional, and negligence. Each type of action is discussed in turn.

Intentional Torts: Assault and Battery

An intentional tort occurs when one individual deliberately interferes with another, resulting in harm. Intent to harm is not necessary to establish tort liability. An intentional tort usually involves allegations of assault and battery or false imprisonment. Cases of intentional injury by school personnel in the school setting are quite rare.

Assault and battery are the most common intentional tort actions filed against school personnel. An assault is a nonphysical act that puts another person in fear of immediate bodily harm. Essentially, an assault is an invasion of a person's peace of mind or space, not a physical attack upon an individual's body. An assault may be committed without actually touching, striking, or doing bodily harm to an individual (*Black's*, 1999). However, the individual who is assaulted has reasonable ground to fear immediate harm and knows that the offender has the ability to carry out the harm that is threatened. Assault may involve words, actions, or both. Assault may be prosecuted under criminal statutes, as well as under civil tort law.

A battery is intentional physical contact that causes bodily injury. Battery begins where assault leaves off. Like assault, battery may be prosecuted under criminal statutes, as well as civil tort law. To threaten to injure another person is an assault; actually hitting another person is battery, which always includes an assault. As a result, the two terms are commonly combined in the phrase "assault and battery" (*Black's*, 1999).

In cases in which a teacher disciplined a student, the most common basis for assault and battery in schools, courts have typically assumed that the teacher was reasonable and within the scope of his or her duty, unless proven otherwise (Alexander & Alexander, 2001).

Intentional Torts: Defamation

Defamation is an intentional action in the form of written or spoken communication that harms a person's reputation or exposes the individual to contempt, hatred, scorn, or ridicule. In addition, it may cause a person to be shunned or avoided, or it may result in harm to a person's employment or business. To constitute defamation, the communication must be false and communicated to a third person. Redress for injury to reputation is a cherished legal right and, contrary to common belief, children and students are not barred from asserting this right.

Teachers, by the very nature of the profession, come into possession of critical, often very personal, information about students and parents. For example, each student has a cumulative folder that contains information about a student's achievement in class, test scores, and disciplinary record. Also included in the "cum" folder may be personal information about the student and family that is gleaned from parent conferences. Some of this information could be communicated to others in such a way as to justify a tort action alleging defamation. The major defense in defamation charges is authorization of school personnel to use information accompanied by special protection against liability. A defense against defamation depends upon showing that the information is true and that malice was not present (Menacker, 1987).

In evaluating a complaint of defamation, courts pose a series of questions. First, was the statement presented as an opinion or as fact? A California teacher brought suit against a school district for defamation after the school's student newspaper published a story about a smoke bomb explosion in which students were quoted as stating that a teacher was a "babbler" and the "worst teacher" at the school. The state appeals court held that these statements were not actionable as libel, reasoning that the statements constituted student expressions of a subjective judgement, protected by the First Amendment, not factual assertions capable of being proven true or false (*Moyer v. Amador Valley Joint Union High School District*, 1990).

Strict Liability

Strict liability involves intentional behavior that causes harm. There is no need to prove fault. Strict liability results when an injury results from the creation of an unusual hazard. An example is an injury resulting from an unfenced construction site or storage of flammable materials in an unlocked area. In this tort action, the plaintiff need not establish that the injury was knowingly or negligently caused. Tort actions based on an allegation of strict liability are rarely brought against a school district.

Educational Malpractice

Until recent times, almost all cases filed against school districts for inappropriate instruction and appealed to a higher court involved physical harm to the student, rather than harm to the intellect. To prevail in an action for physical harm, a plaintiff must show that a teacher failed to exercise his or her duty to provide adequate and appropriate instruction prior to commencing an activity that may pose a risk of harm.

In the last couple of decades, however, students have brought suits against teachers based on alleged malpractice that deprived the student of learning or educational achievement. The concept of educational malpractice in this sense, like the better-known charges of malpractice in the medical and legal professions, is based on negligence in the application of professional skills and knowledge. Such a claim for educational malpractice is an attempt to use tort law to seek compensation when a student who has been through an educational program has failed to attain a certain level of achievement; for example, a student may have been awarded a high school diploma, but cannot read.

The same criteria apply for a plaintiff to prevail in an educational malpractice suit as apply to other tort suits:

- The school district and/or teacher owe the student an obligation that is recognized under the law.
- The standard of care required to fulfill this obligation was breached.
- The school district's or teacher's breach of this duty was the proximate cause of injury to the student.
- The student suffered an actual injury or harm.

One of the first educational malpractice claims was *Peter W. v. San Francisco Unified School District* (1976). Peter was passed from grade to grade and graduated from high school even though his reading ability was at the fifth-grade level and his mathematics ability was also low. At the time, California law required that high school students pass a proficiency test certifying that they could function at or above the eighth grade level.

Peter, an 18-year-old graduate of the district, claimed he was not provided with the basic academic skills he should have acquired during 12 years of school attendance. He alleged that teachers and administrators had failed to diagnose his reading disabilities, placed him in classes that were beyond his capabilities, and allowed him to graduate without ability to read at the eighth-grade level, as required by state law. Peter sought damages sufficient to compensate him for permanent disability and inability to gain meaningful employment, both as a result of the district's failure to exercise its duty of care. In that situation, an appellate court dismissed the student's negligence claims based on grounds of budget restrictions and public policy principles that included:

- the difficulty of establishing a standard of care by which to measure educators' conduct
- lack of a reasonable degree of certainty the student suffered harm as defined by the meaning of negligence law
- lack of an identifiable connection between the educator's conduct and the alleged injury to establish a causal link between the two.

The court determined that three of the four negligence elements were not present in this student's educational malpractice claim. Finally, the court refused to recognize educational malpractice claims because they would expose educators to tort claims by students and parents in countless numbers.

Although districts and individual teachers should be concerned about this type of suit, plaintiffs bringing such suits have met with little success (Hartmeister, 1995).

Constitutional Torts

A Constitutional tort occurs when a person has been deprived of his or her civil rights under either the U.S. Constitution or other federal law. After the Civil War, Congress sought to provide legal redress to African-Americans who had been mistreated by the government. This concern resulted in passage of the Civil Rights Act of 1871 to protect an individual's constitutional and civil rights. This act provided an avenue for suing school boards, individual board members, school administrators, and teachers for monetary damages following denial or deprivation of protected rights such as an individual's rights to due process, equal protection under the law, or freedom of speech.

Negligence Torts

The vast majority of tort cases against educational agencies and their employees have focused on allegations of negligence. Negligence is defined as "failure to exercise the standard of care that a reasonably prudent person would have exercised in a similar situation" (*Black's*, 1999). Negligence differs from an intentional tort in that negligent acts are neither expected nor intended. Many student injury lawsuits involve allegations of administrator or teacher negligence.

In California, Section 1714 of the Civil Code provides,

> Everyone is responsible, not only for the result of his lawful acts, but also for an injury occasioned to another by his want of ordinary care or skill in the management of his property or person, except so far as the latter has, willfully or by the want of ordinary care, brought the injury upon himself.

This statute is the key to California's negligence law. In order to find negligence on the part of a defendant, California courts have held that the following four factors must be present:

- The defendant must have a duty of care to the plaintiff.
- There must have been negligence constituting a breach of that duty.
- There must be an injury to the plaintiff.
- The injury must have occurred as a proximate, or legal, result of the defendant's negligence (*Peter W. v. San Francisco Unified School District,* 1976).

Duty, actual injury, and proximate cause are usually matters of fact and not open to subjective judgement. Should there be any question about these issues in negligence cases, the jury is called to decide upon the facts, being guided by the judge on applicable law. The major task for a plaintiff is to prove that the district or employee breached its duty by failure to exercise a reasonable standard of care.

Duty to the Plaintiff: An injured student usually has little difficulty in proving that the district owes a duty of care to him or her.

Breach of Duty: The second, and most important, issue is whether the teacher, administrator, or district failed to meet its duty of care. This issue has two facets: "standard of care" and "proper supervision."

"Standard of care" requires a plaintiff to show that the defendant failed to act as a "reasonably prudent person" would have acted, given the circumstances. In this sense, a "reasonable person" is considered to be a fictional being of normal intelligence, normal perception, and possessing the physical attributes of the defendant (Hartmeister, 1995). Courts have required, in order to establish a causal relationship between breach of duty and an injury, that an accident or injury must have been foreseeable. School employees will not be held liable when they could not have foreseen, in the reasonable exercise of their legal duty to a student, the injurious consequences of an activity or action.

"Proper supervision" is often at issue when a court weighs an allegation of breach of duty. There is no absolute rule for defining proper supervision because the facts in each case are different. In general, school administrators and teachers are under a duty to exercise only the degree of reasonable care and supervision that a parent of ordinary prudence would have exercised under similar circumstances. Two principles govern supervision:

- Do not create danger through negligent conduct.
- Avoid foreseeable hazards created by others (Hartmeister, 1995).

An example of a court's interpretation of proper supervision is found in the 1970 case of *Dailey v. Los Angeles Unified School District* (1970). In this case, Michael Dailey, a 16-year old student, was "slap boxing" with another student in the boys' gymnasium. The event occurred during recess and lasted for five to ten minutes. About 30 students were watching the two boys fight. Suddenly, after being slapped, Michael fell backward and fractured his skull on the pavement. A short time later, he died. Michael's parents filed a wrongful death action for damages, alleging that the district had failed to supervise the students and that this failure caused their son's death.

During the trial, it was determined that the physical education department was responsible for supervising the gymnasium. The chair of that department stated that he did not know he was to assign a teacher to supervise on any particular day, and there was no formal schedule of supervision times. At the time of the incident, the chair of the department was in the office playing bridge!

The court found that the district had failed to meet the standard of care, and that this failure resulted in Michael's death. *Dailey* illustrates an increasing willingness on the part of the courts to impose upon districts a duty of care to protect students from harm.

Proximate Cause: For liability to be assessed, negligent conduct of school personnel must be the proximate or legal cause of a student's injury. Proximate cause means there is a substantial causal connection between the alleged misconduct and the resulting injury. Did the employee's action or failure to act cause an injury or allow it to happen? The relationship between the employee's behavior and the injury must have been close in time and foreseeable. Foreseeability implies that the employee both could and should have anticipated the potentially dangerous consequences of his or her action or inaction.

School administrators and teachers are expected to establish classroom and school standards that will result in a safe environment in which injuries to students are kept to a minimum. They are also expected to have reasonable foresight in anticipating that an injury may occur. For example, on a very warm day, in a classroom that did not have air conditioning, a teacher decided to conduct class on the school lawn. While there, a boy was playing with a knife by flipping it into the ground. The knife hit another student, injuring his eye. The court held that the teacher should have been able to predict that this dangerous practice would result in injury. His failure to stop it amounted to a breach of the duty of care owed to his students (*Lilienthal v. San Leandro Unified School District*, 1956). Today, no sharp instrument or weapon is allowed on school grounds.

A second case illustrates the necessity for school principals and teachers to foresee the possibility of an accident. At a school site in Tulare, California, a piano was kept in the high school gymnasium and moved from room to room on a dolly. The piano was not attached to the dolly; it just rested on it. One day, the piano toppled over and pinned a girl's ankle to the floor. The court said that school officials should have noticed the possibility of danger and taken steps to prevent injury to students. Consequently, the district was held liable (*Dawson v. Tulare Union District*, 1929).

Situations Requiring Supervision of Students

As a rule of thumb, school districts are responsible for student supervision when a student is traveling to and from school, attending school, or at any school-sponsored activity. The most common supervisory situations follow.

Classrooms and Corridors

Obviously, teachers and administrators have a paramount duty to supervise students in classrooms and school corridors. A serious question arises when a teacher leaves the classroom and students unattended. If a student is injured during the teacher's absence, the teacher and the district are at risk for a tort action. However, temporary teacher absence or distraction from the classroom or from the location of an accident does not automatically amount to negligence in supervision (Valente, 1998). When a student is injured during absence of a teacher from the classroom, the court must decide whether the absence was reasonable or negligent. Nevertheless, teachers risk being charged with negligence if they leave a class unsupervised, and a child is injured.

Athletics, Physical Education, and Playgrounds

Approximately seven million students participate in some type of interscholastic sport during a school year (Stanitski, 1989). A 1989 article in *Education Week* ("Dimensions," 1989) estimated that 36% of secondary school football players incurred at least one injury during the 1988 season. Of these, 60% occurred during practice.

California Government Code section 831.7 provides immunity to a public entity for injuries sustained by any person while participating in a hazardous recreation activity, especially when the injury is an inherent risk of the sport. In spite of this protection for school districts and employees, coaches are favorite targets of lawsuits relating to injuries sustained by students and other members of the general public (Port, 1998). The bulk of lawsuits focus on failure or lack of supervision, but plaintiffs have also alleged inadequate or improper medical care, improper training, and improper instruction.

The majority of playground injuries occur when children fall from playground equipment (Shoop & Dunklee, 1992). Although asphalt is commonly seen in playground areas, a fall from swings or other equipment to asphalt often results in injury. Districts would be prudent to place other materials—such as wood chips, bark, or shredded tires—under playground equipment. These materials pose another risk, as students are often tempted to throw the wood chips or bark, leading to injury. However, a fall to these resilient surfaces is less likely to result in serious injury than a fall to asphalt or cement.

Equipment and Materials

An area of the educational program that frequently gives rise to allegations of improper instruction is school activities that require the use of equipment. It is not expected that every possible danger be predicted or every minor defect corrected immediately; however, all school personnel share a common responsibility to keep school equipment and facilities reasonably safe.

California Government Code section 835 provides that a public entity is liable for injury caused by a dangerous condition of its property if the plaintiff establishes that a piece of equipment or facility was in a dangerous condition at the time of the injury. This code makes it clear that school employees are responsible to inspect the school environment regularly and to correct any known hazards.

A case in point occurred in Conejo Valley in southern California when a child was struck by a car while standing in an area next to the school parking lot that had been designated by the school. The plaintiff established that the lot was small, congested, and known by the district to be a hazard. The court upheld a jury finding, based on the dangerous condition of the property, that the district was liable. The court pointed out that a special relationship exists between a school district and its students such that, although the district cannot ensure complete safety of students, it has a heightened duty to make the school safe (*Constantinescu v. Conejo Valley Unified School District*, 1993).

Lunch Time

The lunch period is a time when school officials are required to be particularly alert for possible injury to a student. Lunch supervision is a challenging time for the school administrator. Education Code section 44813 provides a duty-free lunch period for teachers, who are, consequently, unavailable for supervision. However, this requirement does not free the district from responsibility for adequate supervision of students during the lunch period.

For example, a seven-year-old student was served a hot lunch at school. He was reprimanded for loud and boisterous behavior and was sitting down when he inadvertently knocked his luncheon plate over and spilled hot mashed potatoes onto his lap and down his leg. He suffered second degree burns on a large portion of his leg. The court stated that the district breached its duty of care to protect and supervise the children when it served excessively hot food (*Espinosa v. Fresno Unified School District,* 1992).

Errands

It is common practice for teachers, counselors, and principals to send students on errands. If a student is then injured, the legal question becomes whether the school employee acted reasonably in sending the student on the errand. What constitutes reasonable action depends on the circumstances of each case. As with other examples of negligence, the teacher or principal may be held liable if, in sending a student on an errand, the child is exposed to a danger that should have been apparent to a reasonable and prudent person.

Field Trips and Other Off-Campus Activities

Field trips are school-related activities that take place away from school grounds. Districts owe the same duty of care and supervision to students who participate in field trips, whether mandatory or voluntary, as they do to students during the normal school day on campus. As a general rule, students are subject to a greater risk of injury while on a field trip than during a normal school day. The factors that contribute to greater risk may include being transported in a bus or private vehicle, walking along a busy street, and not following usual classroom and school procedures.

Many school districts require a teacher to complete a field trip application form and obtain parent permission for students to participate in a field trip. However, as discussed earlier, even a parent's written permission may not absolve the district from liability if a student is injured while on the trip. The best defense on a field trip is adequate supervision.

Transportation

When a district provides student transportation, it follows that the district is obligated to provide this transportation in a safe and supervised manner. When a child is injured while being transported, the plaintiff's case usually relies on one or more of three grounds: (a) unsafe equipment, (b) negligent bus operation, or (c) negligent supervision of students at bus stops. Courts have stressed the need for special supervision at bus stops where the potential for accident is greatest.

A major potential for tort action against a school district or employee arises when arrangements are made to transport students in a private vehicle. Should an accident occur, the safety of the vehicle, the proficiency of the driver, and whether the employee was acting as an agent of the district will need to be decided.

Before and After School

Education Code section 44808 is very specific in stating that "no school district . . . shall be responsible or in any way liable for the conduct or safety of any pupil . . . at any time when such pupil is not on school property." There are exceptions, however. As discussed earlier, if a school district provides student transportation or sponsors school activities off campus, the district is responsible for immediate and direct supervision of students and liable for their safety.

Even with this very specific limitation on a district's responsibility for student safety, the duty to provide supervision may extend to times and locations beyond the school day and the campus. For example, although parents and students are regularly notified of the periods in which school is open and supervision is available, a principal's knowledge that students are utilizing school grounds prior to or after the school day may raise an issue as to whether a duty of supervision is created.

Courts impose reasonable limits on the scope of supervisory responsibility. A California Court of Appeals ruled that school officials did not have a duty to scout the neighborhood for gang members before releasing students at the end of the school day, even though school personnel were aware of the presence of gang members near the school during the school day (*Brownell v. Los Angeles Unified School District*, 1992).

In the *Brownell* case, a student was shot by a gang member immediately after school was dismissed. The shooting took place on a public street adjacent to school property. The student sued the school district, alleging negligent supervision because school personnel had dismissed the students after school without first ascertaining whether the street in front of the school was free of any gang members. The student claimed that the Education Code requires teachers to supervise students going to and from school. The court ruled that, under the circumstances, school personnel had exercised due care in their supervision responsibilities to protect students from gang violence by taking such general measures as prohibiting the wearing of gang colors.

Liability is limited in specified undertakings when the pupil is or should be under the immediate and direct supervision of a district employee. However, the courts have ruled in favor of students when they have determined that the district failed to exercise reasonable care under the circumstances of the case. Such a case went to trial after a ten-year-old boy left school during the middle of the day without parent or school permission. While off campus, he was struck by a motorcycle and badly injured. The California Supreme Court held the district liable because of its negligent supervision of the student. The court stated that if the student had been properly supervised, he would not have been allowed to leave school (*Hoyem v. Manhattan Beach City School District*, 1978).

Defenses Against Negligence

In an ideal world there would be no need for a district to protect itself against charges of negligence. However, even if every employee were to exercise the utmost caution in supervising students and every piece of district equipment were in perfect order, accidents would still happen, errors would still be made, and students would sometimes misbehave. In many instances such accidents, mistakes, and misbehavior give rise to lawsuits. On what basis, then, may a district, teacher, administrator, or staff member mount a defense?

Governmental Immunity

While the defense of governmental immunity is disappearing in most states, it once was a common practice. This type of defense is grounded in the traditional concept that "the king can do no wrong." Historically, the government could not be sued without its permission. It was immune.

The immunity rule has eroded or been abrogated in a growing number of states, although a small number of states still maintain the doctrine. Some states maintain the concept of immunity for certain classes of injury, while allowing liability claims for other classes. The erosion of the immunity rule has occurred sometimes by court decision and sometimes by legislation.

California's Personal Liability Law

Although some states still maintain the right of governmental immunity, at least to some degree, California no longer claims this line of defense. Government Code sections 810-996 give citizens the right to bring a tort action against the state or other government entity. The statute contains requirements for filing a claim and timelines that must be strictly adhered to by a party desirous of suing a public agency. For example, Government Code section 911.2 requires a claimant to file a claim for death or injury to person or property within six months of the occurrence and any other claims within a year. The Government Code also contains claim rejection and denial procedures that must be followed to the letter.

However, in spite of the restrictions placed on the claimant, California school districts may be held liable for their tortuous acts where employees or school officials have acted in a negligent manner. California public employees, including teachers, are liable for injury caused by their acts or omissions to the same extent as private persons (Government Code section 820). They may be personally liable if, in the performance of their school duties, their negligent or wrongful conduct causes harm to pupils or others.

The California Tort Claims Act is very specific in that, for a district to be held liable, its employee must have acted within the scope of his or her employment. Under this act, school districts have been found liable for the failure of their employees to use reasonable care to prevent foreseeable injuries resulting from school activities. Districts have also been found liable for improperly supervising students and failure to correct or warn injury victims of known dangerous conditions (Port, 1998).

Teachers face the risk of lawsuits for torts such as assault and battery, slander, libel, defamation, false arrest, and malpractice. However, Government Code section 825 requires a school district to provide a defense and pay any judgment or settlement resulting from an employee's action in the course and scope of employment. In addition, school districts are required to insure against the personal liability of employees for loss or damage to property or damages for death or injury to any person as a result of any negligent act of employees within the scope of their employment (Education Code section 35208). Obviously, however, school employees can be held *personally* liable for injuries resulting from negligent action or inaction outside the course and scope of employment or as a result of fraud, corruption, or malice (*Johnson v. State of California*, 1968).

Contributory Negligence

In defending against a negligence claim, a district may be able to demonstrate that the injured student's own conduct contributed to his or her injury. Just as the court will examine what a reasonable or prudent teacher or staff member would do in a given situation, the court will consider what a reasonable or prudent student or parent would have done for his or her own protection. Whether an injured child can be contributorily negligent in a given situation usually depends on the age and maturity of the child. If a child is too young to understand the danger of his or her act, the child cannot be held to have contributed to the injury.

Comparative Negligence

A defense of comparative negligence is viable when it can be shown that an injury was partly the fault of several persons. Under the comparative negligence doctrine, all of the parties, including the plaintiff, are liable for their respective shares of the plaintiff's loss or injury, and liability is assessed in direct proportion to fault.

Assumption of Risk

Under the doctrine of assumption of risk, an injured person is not allowed to recover damages if the person sustains an injury after voluntarily participating in an activity that is known to be inherently dangerous. The legal theory is based upon an individual's ability to understand and appreciate the dangers inherent in the activity. The defense must show that the student understood the danger, knew the risk involved, and accepted the danger. Athletic activities are an example of the assumption of risk doctrine. This doctrine may protect coaches and school administrators from liability on the grounds that students who voluntarily participate in school athletic programs assume some risk.

Notice of Claim

Most states have very specific timelines within which an injured party must file a tort claim. The timeline requires a plaintiff to file a claim within three to six months of the injury. These statutes describe how the legitimacy of tort claims is to be validated, provide for notice to the district to correct conditions that could result in additional injury, and give the district an opportunity to budget sufficient funds to employ legal defense and pay compensation, if awarded. Some states also set specific dollar ceilings for the several classes of tort claims. These ceilings range from a modest amount of several thousand dollars to several hundred thousand dollars.

Written Waivers

Parental consent for student participation in special activities, such as field trips and athletic competition, is often required. School forms for this purpose include a declaration that the parent releases the school and its personnel from all legal responsibility for any injury the child may suffer while participating in the special event. While a release form offers a district limited protection from a civil suit, some courts hold that a parent cannot legally surrender the independent claim of a minor child.

Compensation

To receive an award of damages or compensation, a plaintiff must have suffered an injury from the negligent conduct of the defendant. Although the defendant's conduct may be considered negligent, legal action cannot be sustained unless the conduct actually results in physical or mental injury. Compensation may cover any direct financial loss, for example, medical expenses or loss of income. Compensation for pain and suffering may also be awarded.

Several different kinds of damage may be sought by injured students as plaintiffs in a lawsuit. The most common types are:

Compensatory Damages: Damages that compensate an injured party for actual losses. These include medical expenses, lost salary, court costs, or compensation for physical or mental injuries to a person.

Punitive or Exemplary Damages: Damages awarded for the purpose of punishing the defendant for negligence. The plaintiff must prove evidence of violence, oppression, malice, fraud, or wanton or reckless disregard for the plaintiff's safety. Punitive damages are intended to prevent or deter defendants from doing the same thing again.

Nominal Damages: Limited monetary awards, given by a court or jury when there is technically little or no actual loss, but the plaintiff nonetheless has been mistreated.

Monetary damages are the legal system's way of making a plaintiff "whole again," and to compensate a person who has suffered loss to his person, property, or rights through unlawful acts of another.

Summary

The school district and its personnel have a legal duty to protect students, employees, and visitors from unreasonable risks of injury. A reasonable and prudent school administrator, teacher, or school employee is expected to foresee potential dangers in the school environment, anticipate the injurious consequences of actions, and take appropriate steps to reduce risks. The law requires school leaders to meet a standard of reasonable, prudent care for the safety of students. Since school officials serve as surrogate parents, a general duty to provide adequate supervision is consistently imposed by the courts. The obligation of district personnel to provide a safe environment at all times is serious and constant.

Off-campus activities, such as athletic events and field trips, should be carefully planned and evaluated from both an educational and a safety viewpoint. To establish an appropriate level of supervision, the teacher and principal should take into account the age and maturity of students.

Courts have generally held school districts and employees liable for injury to students during the course of regular school events if there has been failure to provide a reasonably safe environment. School employees also have a moral, professional, and legal obligation to warn students of known hazards, to remove known dangers, and to instruct students properly when they participate in school activities. Educators must be knowledgeable about their potential liability and should take care to have adequate insurance protection to cover any awards that might be assessed against them.

Key Terms

1. assault
2. assumption of risk
3. battery
4. breach of duty
5. comparative negligence
6. compensatory damages
7. Constitutional tort
8. contributory negligence
9. educational malpractice
10. exemplary damages
11. governmental immunity
12. intentional tort
13. negligence
14. notice of claim
15. proximate cause
16. punitive damages
17. standard of care
18. strict liability
19. tort
20. written waiver

Discussion / Essay Questions

1. Discuss the major differences between a criminal suit and a tort suit.

2. Tort actions can be divided into five major categories. Which is the most likely to occur in the school setting? Why is that the case?

3. School employees are responsible for observing the standard of care for students under their supervision. What does this concept mean? Give examples.

4. As a general principle, school districts are not legally responsible for accidents that occur before students arrive at school in the morning or after they have been released in the afternoon. Describe situations to which this principle does *not* apply.

5. It appears that malpractice suits against teachers will increase. Discuss several ways you believe teachers can protect themselves from this type of lawsuit.

6. Governmental immunity has protected governmental agencies, including school districts, from tort actions. California does not permit this defense. Do you agree with California's position? State reasons for your position.

References

Alexander, K., & Alexander, M. D. (2001). *American public school law* (5th ed.). Belmont, CA: West/Thomson Learning.

Black's Law Dictionary (7th ed.). (1999). Bryan A. Garner, Editor-in-Chief. St. Paul, MN: West Group.

Dimensions: High school football injuries. (1989). *Education Week, 8,* 3.

Hartmeister, F. (1995). *Surviving as a teacher: The legal dimension.* Chicago, IL: Precept Press.

Irvine, M. (1996, October 3). School may fight $500,000 award in harassment case. *Orange County Register,* p. 31.

Menacker, J. (1987). *School law: Theoretical and case perspectives.* Englewood Cliffs, NJ: Prentice-Hall.

Port, L. (1998). *Between a rock and a hard place; Law for school administrators.* Foster City, CA: School Law Publishers.

School settles with gay man for abuse. (1996, November 21). *Los Angeles Times.*

Shoop, R., & Dunklee, D. (1992). *School law for the principal: A handbook for practitioners.* Needham Heights, MA: Allyn & Bacon.

Stanitski, C. (1989). Common injuries in pre-adolescent and adolescent athletics. *Sports Medicine*, *7*, 32-33.

Valente, W. (1998). *Law and the schools* (4th ed.). NY: Macmillan.

Court Cases

Brownell v. Los Angeles Unified School District, 4 Cal.App.4th 791, 5 Cal.Rptr.2d 756 (1992)

Constantinescu v. Conejo Valley Unified School District, 16 Cal.App..4th 1466, 20 Cal.Rptr.2d, 734 (1993)

Dailey v. Los Angeles Unified School District, Ca. Sup.Ct., 2 Cal. 3d 741, 87 Cal.Rptr 376, 470 p.2d 360 (1970)

Dawson v. Tulare Union District, 276 Pac. 424, 98 Cal. App 138 (Calif. 1929)

Espinosa v. Fresno Unified School District, 5 Cal.App.. 4th 889 (1992)

Hoyem v. Manhattan Beach City School District, 22 Cal.3d, 508, 150 Cal.Rptr. 1 (1978)

Johnson v. State of California, 69 Cal.2d 782, 73 Cal.Rptr. 240 (1968)

Lilienthal v. San Leandro Unified School District, 293 P.2d 889, 139 Cal.App., 2nd 453 (1956)

Moyer v. Amador Valley Joint Union High School District, 225 Cal.App.. 3d, 720 (1990)

Peter W. v. San Francisco Unified School District, 60 Cal.App.. 3d 817, 131 Cal.Rptr. 854 (1976)

INDEX